NG TO TELL YOU
ET. SOMETHING FOR
EARS ONLY—
Y REAL
NAME."
Hick
BELOVED.
ONE WHO IS ADORED.
"DON'T FORGET."
AS IF I COULD EVER FORGET WHEN ERASURE IS THE THING I FEAR MOST.
...SEIMEI...
...WAS DEAD.
YOU WON'T.
ONE WEEK AFTER I HEARD THAT BEAUTIFUL NAME...
HOW COULD I FORGET?
Hun?
For me?
Just me?
BUMP
BUMP

CHAPTER 1

LOVE

(I WONDERED WHAT HE MEANT BY "REAL NAME," BUT...)
IT WAS FITTING, SINCE EVERYONE LOVED SEIMEI.

BUT SEIMEI DIED.
HE DIED IN AN UNIMAGINABLE WAY.

GOOD MORNING.
CHAK
I'M RITSUKA AOYAGI.

KTUNK
OH!
YOU'RE AOYAGI?
OH, GOOD MORNING. ♡
HI.
UM, WHERE ARE YOUR PARENTS?
THEY'RE BUSY PEOPLE.
THEY COULDN'T MAKE IT.
SMILE
HUH?
B...
BUSY? BUT...
THIS IS YOUR FIRST DAY AS A TRANSFER STUDENT ...
I BROUGHT MY OWN PAPER-WORK.
YOU CAME BY YOUR-SELF...?
SIXTH GRADERS CAN GET TO SCHOOL ON THEIR OWN.
THAT'S NORMAL.
FLICK
FLICK

DON'T WORRY.
I'M USED TO THIS.
OH.
AO-YAGI ...
MS. SHINO-NOME.
PLENTY OF KIDS COME FROM HOMES LIKE MINE.
IT DOESN'T BOTHER ME.
MY HOME-ROOM IS NUMBER 3, RIGHT?
LET'S GO!
SHKLAK
OH!!
EXCUSE US!
AOYAGI!
HE'S SUCH A...
MURMUR
...STRONG YOUNG BOY.
SAYING HE'S USED TO IT AND ALL.
YES, AND...
HE HAS A BIT OF A PAST.
HOW SO?
YANO JONAN ELEMENTARY SCHOOL
RITSUKA AOYAGI
THERE ARE TROUBLING COMMENTS IN THE FILE FROM HIS OLD SCHOOL.
YOU WON'T BELIEVE THEM.
MURMUR
OH MY!
OH, THAT!
THAT WAS IN THE NEWS.

RITSUKA AOYAGI.
SAME AOYAGI AS THAT INCIDENT.
YANO JONAN ELEMENTARY SCHOOL
RITSUKA AOYAGI
POOR BOY, I HOPE HE'S NOT TRAUMATIZED.
AND THOSE BRUISES...
HE'LL TAKE A DELICATE TOUCH.
CAN MS. SHINONOME HANDLE THIS?
SHE'S A LITTLE... WELL... YOU KNOW.
NOVEMBER 17
RITSUKA
•Daily Duties: Sakurada, Tayama
BDMP
BDMP
BDMP
AOYAGI
This week's goals: Memorize script

SAY HELLO TO RITSUKA AOYAGI!
HI.
NICE TO MEET YOU.
WOW!
RITSUKA? HE'S SO COOL!!
WHAT-EVER.
LOOKS AVERAGE TO ME.
PING!
HEY, YUIKO. WHY DON'TCHA TALK TO HIM LATER?
WHAT?
YUIKO'S TOO SHY!!
THEN WHY'D YOU SHOUT ABOUT HIM BEING COOL?
ERGH–
NO!
OKAY!
LET'S BEGIN!
NO!
START FROM PAGE 46 OF YOUR TEXT-BOOKS.
WOW... HUGE BOOBS.
Looks...
...kinda dumb.
HI.
BLUSH
N...

H...
HERE!!
WHAM
'KAY.
For me?
We could just share...
HE'S...
She's a weirdo.
CAN I SEE YOUR TEXT-BOOK?
HE'S SITTING NEXT TO ME!!
SKRUT
...
NO.
I DON'T.
What?
UH...
SOME-THING...
GOTTA SAY SOMETHING!
BDMP
BDMP
SORN
BDMP
HEY, RITSUKA, DO YOU HAVE A CELL PHONE?
OH, THEN...
WHO'S YOUR FAVORITE IN MORNING MUSUME?
GOTTA TALK!
YUIKO LIKES GOMAKI!
She's so cute.
HUH?
GOTTA TALK!!
UH, WHERE'S YOUR CRAM SCHOOL?
DON'T GO TO ONE.
TALK...
OH.
'KAY.
WELL THEN...

THERE'S TOO MANY. I CAN'T TELL THEM APART.
WHAAAAT?
FLICK
THEN WHY ASK ABOUT STUFF LIKE THAT?
OH! WELL, YOU'RE SO COOL!
YUIKO THINKS EVERYONE WANTS TO GET TO KNOW YOU BETTER.
NO WAY.
YOU DON'T KNOW MO-MUSU?
LOOK.
THAT SO?
A moron for sure.
BLUSH
SO I'M "COOL"?
HUH?
WHY ARE YOU INTER-ROGATING ME?
BECAUSE EVERYONE TOLD YUIKO TO TALK TO YOU.
FLAIL
FLAIL
FLAIL
YOU DUMMY! WE DIDN'T SAY THAT!
YOU'RE THE ONE WHO SAID HE WAS COOL!
GYAH
NO!
GRR
ALL OF YOU!
IT'S THE MIDDLE OF CLASS!
PEOPLE WHO GET USED BY OTHERS...
STOP!
SKRUT
HUH?

...ARE PATHETIC.
PEOPLE WHO USE OTHERS ARE DUMB, BUT NOT AS DUMB AS THE ONES WHO GET USED.
H-USH...
...
SOB
SO YOU THINK ...
...YUIKO'S DUMB?
I HATE DUMB GIRLS.
HERE'S YOUR BOOK.
FWAP
SIXTH GRADE JAPANESE
PLIP
SIXTH GRADE JAPANESE
WAAAH!!
CRASH
GYAH!!
WHAT A JERK!
I CAN'T BELIEVE HIM!
GYA
GYA
GYA
POOR YUIKO!
HOW COULD YOU MAKE A GIRL CRY?!
HEY, EVERY-ONE! IT'S CLASS TIME!!
CLASS!!

THEY PRETEND TO BE YOUR FRIEND BUT TREAT YOU LIKE A SLAVE.
THE WORLD IS FULL OF PREDATORY PEOPLE.
UNREAL...
DAY ONE AND HE'S ALREADY TURNED ALL THE GIRLS AGAINST HIM.
SEIMEI, LIFE SUCKS.
HE'S EITHER AWESOME...
...OR TOTALLY LAME!!
...IT WOULD HURRY UP AND END.
I WISH...
RITSUKA!
RITSUKA!

HEY, RITSUKA! LUNCH TIME!
DON'T BOTHER WITH HIM, YUIKO!
HE'S A CREEP!
GRR GRR
GRR
FLOP
WHAT? THAT'S NOT TRUE!
Eheh...
Yeah, it is.
YOUR FRIENDS WON'T LIKE IT IF YOU HANG AROUND ME.
CLAK
EHEH... LET'S EAT TOGETHER.
That jerk! Ignore him!
YUIKO LOVES FRIED BREAD!
WHAT DO YOU LIKE TO EAT FOR LUNCH, RITSUKA?
WHATEVER.
Sigh...
HERE I WAS, ENJOYING SOME PEACE AND QUIET... HOW OBNOXIOUS.
CHEWING'S A HASSLE, SO I LIKE SOFT STUFF.
HUH? REALLY?
THAT'S LIKE A GRANDPA.
Grandpa?!
LOOK.
DON'T GO OUT OF YOUR WAY TO TALK TO ME.

YOU REALLY DON'T EVEN TRY, DO YOU?
RITSUKA.
YOU...
What a creep!
NOPE.
I DON'T.
BLUSH
IT'S A HASSLE TO ANSWER ALL THESE QUESTIONS.
WHAT TIME DOES SCHOOL LET OUT?
EXCUSE ME.
BUT WAITING OUTSIDE THE SCHOOL GATE IS THE SUREST BET.
IT'LL LOOK QUESTION-ABLE ...
THANK YOU.
IT'S SATURDAY, SO THEY END AT 12:30.

ffff
BING
BONG

BING BONG
RITSUKA!
GOING HOME?
DOING ANYTHING?
I'VE GOT NO PLANS, SO I'M GOING TO THE LIBRARY.
WHAT? THE SCHOOL LIBRARY?
ELEMENTARY SCHOOLS DON'T HAVE ANY GOOD BOOKS.
SO I'M GOING TO A LIBRARY.
A PUBLIC ONE. FOR ADULTS.
REALLY?!
YUIKO WANTS TO COME!
WE'RE GOING HOME. WHAT ARE YOU DOING, YUIKO?
PING!
CARRY MY BAGS!
HEY!
SORRY, NOT TODAY.
What?
YUIKO'S GOING HOME WITH RITSUKA.
You weren't invited!
GRR—
GRR
GRR
GRR
WHAT'S ALL THAT ABOUT?
YUIKO'S PISSING ME OFF!
LOOK.
IF YOU KEEP THIS UP, THEY'RE GOING TO TURN ON YOU.
IT'S FINE! THEY'RE YUIKO'S FRIENDS.
AND IT'S NOT "LOOK," IT'S YUIKO.

NO THANKS.
Why are idiots so happy?
YUIKO HAWATARI!
SMILE
JUST CALL ME YUIKO!!
YOU KNOW ABOUT ME NOW, DON'T YOU?
I'M FINE.
HAWATARI HERE IS BEING SUPER NICE TO ME.
OH...
TRMBL
HOW WAS YOUR FIRST DAY ?
H...
MS. SHINONOME ?
I'M ALWAYS HERE TO LISTEN.
Huh ?!
WHY ?
WHY ?
WHAT ? HUH ?
WHY NOT? SAY YUIKO!
SAY IT!
SAY IT!
No way!
AO-YAGI !

HUH?
WHAT?
RIT-SUKA!
YOU'RE SUCH A FAKER!
OH.
OKAY!
HUH?
OKAY!
WE'RE GONNA GO TO THE LIBRARY NOW.
THAT'S NICE OF YOU, HAWATARI.
REALLY ?
Ah...
WELL, EXCUSE ME FOR BEING A FAKE!
I JUST CAN'T STAND PEOPLE WORRY-ING ABOUT ME.
YOU'RE SO WEIRD!
HEE HEE
IT'S LIKE YOU'VE GOT A SPLIT PERSON-ALITY, RITSUKA.
BADUMP

SORRY, RITSUKA!
YUIKO'S ...!
LEAVE ME ALONE.
UM.
HUH?
SOR...
DON'T EVER SAY THAT AGAIN!
!
ZING
GO AWAY!
Y...
YUIKO DOESN'T GET IT, BUT...
SORRY!
SPLIT PERSON-ALITY?
IT'S NOT LIKE THAT I'M...
DASH
RITSUKA!
DON'T SAY THAT...

WHAT'S THE MATTER, RITSUKA?
WHY ARE YOU CRYING?
TUG

I'M NOT CRYING, YOU JERK!
YOU.
GRRR
WHO THE HELL ARE YOU?!
LET GO OF MY ARM!
WHA ...?!
WHO'S CRYING?!
YOU DON'T KNOW ME?
WHY SHOULD I?
LET ME GO!
WHOA...
THIS GUY...
FLICK
SO I CAME FOR YOU INSTEAD.
YOU NEVER CAME FOR ME, RITSUKA.

HE DOESN'T HAVE EARS.
LET GO OF ME!
RIP
HISS
HOW DO YOU KNOW MY NAME?
WHO ARE YOU?!
HISS
He's an adult.
A KIDNAP-PER?!
A PERVERT ?!
HISS
He gives me the creeps!
HE'S AN ADULT!!
NOT VERY TRUSTING, IS HE?
I'M A FIGHTER.
SEIMEI NEVER TOLD YOU...
...ABOUT ME?
Sounds fishy.
HUH?!
HISS
HISS
WELL... THIS IS AWKWARD.

YOU'RE SEIMEI'S ...
YOU KNEW MY BROTHER ?
YES.
YOU'RE SEIMEI'S FRIEND?
BUT YOU NEVER CAME BY OUR HOUSE, RIGHT? I'D HAVE REMEMBERED THAT.
OH...
WHAT'S YOUR NAME?
SOUBI.
YOU CAME TO SEE ME, SOUBI?
Yes.
BUT WHY?

HEY, ARE YOU BUSY RIGHT NOW?
HUG
LET'S GO MAKE SOME MEMORIES!
BLUSH
SHWUF...
WHATEVER YOU WANT, RITSUKA.
ANR-UH-!
LET'S.

ALL RIGHT.
OKAY.
SAY CHEESE!
SONY! VS/OPTICAL 4X
f=8-24mm
GA PIXELS!
CLICK
PING!
KINU
THANK YOU, LADY! ♡
OH! DON'T MENTION IT.
AWE-SOME! WE TOOK A TON OF PICTURES.
SO!
THIS IS MAKING MEMORIES ?
THAT'S RIGHT. I'LL PRINT THEM LATER.
YOU BETTER NOT THROW THEM OUT, SOUBI!
HUFF
HUFF
KINUTA PA

OF COURSE NOT! I WOULD NEVER FORGET.
YOU WILL.
YOU FORGET WITHOUT PHOTOS. SO WE HAVE TO TAKE PICTURES FIRST.
FWUMP
OTHERWISE YOU'LL JUST FORGET I WAS EVER HERE.
THAT SOUNDS LOVELY.
BUT LET'S TALK SOME MORE.
WON'T THAT MAKE FOR BETTER MEMORIES?
NUH-UH!
BUT...
IT'S ALL RIGHT.
IT CAN'T BE HELPED.
RIT-SUKA...
JUST WHAT KIND OF KID IS HE...?
I ONLY LEARNED HIS NAME AND HIS FACE.
HE'S SEIMEI'S BROTHER.

IT'S POINTLESS ...
...TO TRY TO MAKE MEMORIES WITH A STRANGER.
BUT SOUBI, YOU'RE SEIMEI'S FRIEND.
TO ME...
...THAT COUNTS FOR A LOT!
...
BUT...
I NEVER KNEW.
HM?
THAT SEIMEI ...
...HAD AN ADULT FRIEND.
BLUSH
OH.
MY EARS ?
DON'T WORRY. I WON'T DO ANYTHING TO YOU.

I DON'T BELIEVE YOU!
HNGGH
SCREW YOU, SOUBI!
YOU SAID YOU WOULDN'T DO ANY-THING!
IT WAS JUST A KISS.
YOU SAID...
...NOT ANY-THING!

FROM NOW ON, THE TWO OF US...
LEND ME YOUR STRENGTH.
...MUST BE JOINED BY A DEEP BOND, A BOND STRONGER THAN ANY OTHER PAIR.
WORDS LIKE THAT MAKE MY HEAD SPIN.
BOND ?
STOP IT, YOU CAN'T...
STRONG.
DEEP.
FLINCH
...WANT WITH ME?
GRIT
WHAT DO YOU...
...I WILL...
...SEDUCE RITSUKA.
WITH THESE WORDS...

A FIGHTER OTHER THAN MYSELF.
WOOSH
SOME-ONE'S HERE.
THEY'RE CLOSE. SOMEWHERE IN THIS PARK.
WAH!
AI?!
WEEN

WE'VE MADE CONTACT.
SHAAA
ARE YOU OKAY?
YEAH... WE KINDA RAN INTO THEM.
THEY'RE HERE, REALLY CLOSE BY.
RAN INTO THEM?
WH...
WHAT NOW?
DOES...
Urgh
DOES THAT MEAN YOU WANT TO HAVE SEX?

NOT NOW.
GTAK
I COULDN'T GET HARD FOR A CHILD, RITSUKA.
IT'D BE A PROBLEM IF YOU COULD!!
MY MOM WOULD FAINT IF I LOST MY EARS AT MY AGE.
But you kissed me.
That better be the truth.
I heard you say it.
VWIP
VWIP
I HAVEN'T PREPARED RITSUKA YET. WHAT SHOULD I DO?
THERE'S A FIGHTER HERE!!
DOES THIS MEAN WE HAVE TO DO BATTLE? WE WERE JUST TOLD TO BRING HIM IN.
WHAT ?!
AND HE'S...
...REALLY BIG!
THERE'S A FIGHTER HERE!!
THAT KID HAS A FIGHTER WITH HIM, I KNOW IT.
NO ONE SAID ANYTHING ABOUT THIS!

HE'S HERE!!
AND HE'S REALLY ...
...POWER-FUL!
I LOVE YOU...
RITSUKA.
HUH?
WHA ...?!
TWITCH
Don't ...
EXCUSE ME?!
...jerk me around!
I LOVE YOU.
HEH
I'LL PROTECT YOU.
I'LL DO ANYTHING FOR YOU, RITSUKA.
SHIVER...
ANY-THING ...?
ANY-THING!
I GIVE YOU ALL OF ME.

THEY'RE COMING.
MY BODY.
MY HEART.
MY SOUL.
EVERY-THING FOR YOU.
I'D EVEN GIVE YOU MY LIFE.
I'LL FIGHT FOR YOU, RITSUKA.
SO THERE'S NOTHING TO BE AFRAID OF.
HOW CAN YOU...
"AFRAID"?
OF WHAT?
BLUSH
...SAY STUFF LIKE THAT?
I CAN SAY IT...
ALMOST THERE.
...BECAUSE I CAN CAST SPELLS WITH MY WORDS!

HEY!!
VWEEN
YOU!
ZSSH
I AM.
WHO THE HELL ARE YOU?
YOU'RE STILL ALIVE ?!
SOUBI ?!
DON'T TELL ME YOU'RE LOVELESS' FIGHTER!

I WON'T HAND OVER RITSUKA.
BELOVED
BELOVED
"I'LL TELL YOU A SECRET."
BELOVED
YOU...
WHAT WERE YOU TO SEIMEI?
SOUBI...

KNOCK IT OFF! YOU'RE CRAZY!
A FIGHTER CAN'T SERVE TWO MASTERS.
WHAT, SINCE BELOVED IS DEAD, NOW YOU'RE GOING TO SERVE LOVELESS?
THAT'S NOT ALLOWED!
I AM THE FIGHTER FOR BELOVED.
BELOVED
AND NOW I AM YOURS, RITSUKA.
SOUBI.
HE'S SO STRANGE.
ALL THIS IS SO STRANGE.
I CAN'T MAKE SENSE OF IT!..
DON'T WORRY.
I'LL EXPLAIN LATER.
What's going on?
RIT-SUKA.
Some-one explain...

SO WHY...?
ALL HE DID WAS CALL MY NAME...
...AND I'M CRYING.
LOOK WHAT HE'S DONE!
MIDORI, LET ME FIGHT!
HE'S GOT ZERO PRIDE! I CAN'T FORGIVE HIM!
I KNOW. GO AHEAD!
AFTER ALL, THIS IS OUR DUTY.
I DECLARE ...
...A BATTLE BY WORD SPELL.
HE'S MAKING HIS MOVE.
GO.
I ACCEPT!
WE WILL BE ON AUTO-MATIC.
WHAT?!

VWEEN
AUTO-MATIC MEANS ...
EXPAND ...
HUH?
ON AUTO?
BATTLE SYSTEMS.
ARE YOU...
...MOCKING US?!
...ONLY THE FIGHTER BATTLES.
IN OTHER WORDS, IT'S TWO AGAINST ONE.
MIDORI, GIVE ME YOUR HAND!
IF YOU THINK YOU CAN OWN THE NAME ALL BY YOURSELF, GO RIGHT AHEAD!
NOW I'M ANGRY!
FINE THEN!
I'M NOT...
...MOCKING THEM.
WE SHARE THE SAME NAME: BREATH-LESS.
WE ARE OF THE SAME SOUL.

IT'S JUST...
RITSUKA'S NOT READY TO FIGHT YET.
BUT...
breath less
WEEEN
JUST CLOSE YOUR EYES.
I PROMISE.
I WILL PROTECT YOU.
"BREATH-LESS."
WEEEN
IT MEANS ...
...A FORCE THAT WILL TAKE YOUR BREATH AWAY.
EXPAND ...
BATTLE SYSTEMS !
WOON

RIP.
TEAR APART.
YOU'RE ON!
GWO
FULL DEFENSE MODE.
NONE OF YOUR ATTACKS SHALL REACH ME.
ZHK
ZHK
ZHK
SIMPLE SPELLS WON'T CUT IT!
HE'S UP TO FOUR SYLLABLES ALREADY! ALL MY ATTACKS GOT DEFLECTED ...
WHOA!

SHRED.
RIP
RIP
RIP
TEAR UP.
DESTROY.
IT'S NO USE.
ZHK
ZHK
CRUDE SPELLS LIKE THAT WON'T WORK ON ME.
AND NOW...
...SHALL I ATTACK?
MIDORI WILL BE DAMAGED IF I DO.
DON'T LISTEN TO HIM, AI!
I'M YOUR SACRIFICE!
THE WAY THINGS ARE...
!!
YOU CAN'T HESITATE NOW!
I'M SUPPOSED TO BEAR THE DAMAGE! THAT'S HOW THINGS ARE...
...YOU'RE NOT STRONG ENOUGH TO PROTECT MIDORI.

NGH ...!
CALM DOWN, AI.
DON'T LET HIM GET YOU.
HE'S JUST TRYING TO RILE YOU UP.
HEY.
HEY, HEY. HOLD ON.
I DON'T UNDERSTAND WHAT'S GOING ON.
...
DOES THIS MAKE SOUBI THE BAD GUY...?
IS HE THE VILLAIN HERE?!
YOINK
WHOA!
RETREAT.
LEAVE THIS PLACE BEHIND.
Yikes!
So lame. Carrying me!!
WOOOON
HEY!
THAT'S NO FAIR! HE'S RUNNING AWAY?
GRR
AWAY TO A PLACE OF SLEEP.
GRR
NO WAY!
HOLD ON A MINUTE!
GRR
FLY AWAY LIKE TWO LITTLE BIRDS.
HUH?
BIRDS ?!

FWA
FWA
FWA
FWA
YES.
LITTLE BIRDS.
AREN'T THEY?
THOSE TWO, I MEAN.
WHEN I'M FIGHTING, I CAN DO JUST ABOUT ANYTHING...
...BUT SINCE I MADE THE FIRST DECLARATION THIS TIME, I COULDN'T RETREAT.
YOU SEE?
THEY VANISHED!
YES.
SO RETREAT MEANT...
BDMP
BDMP
BDMP

SO I HAD THEM RETREAT INSTEAD.
It's a secret banishment trick.
D...
D...
DID THEY ...
HM? OH NO. I JUST SENT THEM HOME.
...DIE ?
DIE...
WHA...
YOU'RE ADOR-ABLE.
WHAT THE HELL IS THAT ABOUT ?!
RITSUKA, I LOVE YOU.
SHFF
SHFF
WHENEVER YOU'RE IN TROUBLE I'LL ALWAYS COME SAVE YOU. REMEMBER THAT.
HE MAY BE AN ADULT, BUT HE'S SO STRANGE.
PUT ME DOWN ...
LET ME HOLD YOU JUST A LITTLE LONGER.
My ears!
No biting!

THAT WAS THE FIRST TIME...
...ANYONE'S EVER SAID ANYTHING LIKE THAT TO ME.
THEY'RE WHY I'M WILLING TO THROW EVERYTHING AWAY.
RITSUKA, IT'S THOSE EYES.
WHAT?
"SEE YOU"?
HMM
WELL THEN, SEE YOU.
TMP
EYES THAT CAN FORGIVE ANYTHING.
PUT ME DOWN.
THOSE EYES FULL OF YEARNING ...

WAIT...
SOUBI ?!
HE'S GONE?
REALLY ?!
WHAT ?
BUT...
YOU SAID YOU'D EXPLAIN LATER...
SO EXPLAIN, DAMN IT!
CRAP! IT'S 6 O'CLOCK ?
ARGH!
I DON'T BELIEVE THIS!
I'LL MISS MY CURFEW!
FWOO
SOUBI...
BUT...
EVEN SO...
TAK
TAK
I STILL HAVE THOSE 50 PHOTOS IN MY DIGITAL CAMERA.

THIS IS WHY I SAID PHOTOS ARE IMPORTANT.
KREE
KREE
SEE...
SO, ULTIMATELY ...
YOU WERE NOT ABLE TO RETRIEVE LOVELESS, CORRECT?
BUT NOTHING WAS THE WAY YOU SAID IT WOULD BE.
YOU SAID THAT LOVELESS WOULDN'T HAVE A FIGHTER YET.

I ASSUMED IT WOULD GO SMOOTHLY SINCE YOU'RE THE SAME AGE.
HE'S A SIXTH GRADER.
FROM BELOVED.
IT WAS SOUBI.
LOVELESS HAD AN INCREDIBLE FIGHTER WITH HIM.
BUT THE NAME IS DIFFERENT.
I DON'T BELIEVE THAT...
IT WAS SOUBI?
SSHK
THAT CAN'T BE.
!
HE'S A DISGRACE TO ALL FIGHTERS.
SKWEEI
BELOVED DIED, SO HOW COULD HE STILL BE ALIVE?
I WAS PRETTY SHOCKED TOO.
YES?
BREATH-LESS?
...
YOU KNOW YOU CANNOT BRING A FIGHTER HERE.

NO.
THE TWO OF US GO EVERY-WHERE TOGETHER.
SKWEEZ
...
BREATHLESS, WILL YOU TRY AGAIN?
OR...
OF COURSE WE'LL GO.
IT'S WRONG FOR LOVELESS TO CLAIM A FIGHTER WHO ISN'T HIS.
AND IT'S EVEN MORE WRONG OF SOUBI TO TAKE A SECOND SACRIFICE.
THIS TIME WE'LL GET THE JOB DONE!

HOW ARE YOU DOING, RITSUKA?
TIK
TOK
FINE, I GUESS.
TIK
TOK
DID ANYTHING HAPPEN ...
...THIS WEEK?
TOK
TIK
NOT REALLY.
HEY, DR. KATSUKO.
DO THAT THING.
WHAT THING ?
COME ON, YOU KNOW.
THAT HYPNOSIS THING.
HMM...
ALL RIGHT, BUT I DON'T THINK IT WILL WORK THE WAY YOU EXPECT IT TO, RITSUKA.
SKTCH
I KNOW YOU'RE AFRAID.

...HOW SCARED YOU TRULY ARE, RITSUKA.
THE WAY YOU ACT SO TOUGH JUST MASKS...
...MAYBE "RITSUKA" WILL SHOW UP.
IF I CAN GO BACK TWO YEARS...
HOW MANY PERSON-ALITIES ARE WE TALKING ABOUT?
JUST THIS ONE AND THE "RITSUKA AOYAGI" WHO HE WAS FROM BIRTH TO AGE 10.
WHAT ABOUT THE BOY'S MEMORIES ?
HE ONLY HAS ONES FORMED THESE PAST TWO YEARS.
WARD
HE HAS MULTIPLE PERSON-ALITIES ?
TWO YEARS AGO ONE IDENTITY VANISHED AND HASN'T RETURNED.
TO BE SPECIFIC, WE'RE TALKING ABOUT IDENTITIES SWITCHING PLACES.

YOU'RE INJURED.
YEAH.
SWF
DOES IT HURT?
SURE, I GUESS.
BUT IT'S NOTHING I CAN'T DEAL WITH.
DID YOUR MOTHER DO THAT TO YOU?
THOSE INJURIES MUST BE CHILD ABUSE.
WERE YOU BULLIED AT SCHOOL?
HIS MOTHER IS A COMPLETE HYSTERIC.
BUT THE BOY DOESN'T DISPLAY ANY TROUBLESOME BEHAVIOR.
OF COURSE NOT!!
COME ON, DR. KATSUKO, WHAT ABOUT THE HYPNOSIS?

AND YOU'RE FINE WITH THAT?
YEAH.

IF "RITSUKA" APPEARS, YOU TELL HIM FOR ME...
HE CAN HAVE THIS BODY BACK, SO TAKE IT.

SO... RITSUKA.
IF "HE" COMES BACK, WHAT WILL YOU DO?

"HE."
IF...
...

CHAPTER 2

MOM IS WAITING FOR "RITSUKA"...
I SUSPECT THIS TO BE A CASE OF AMNESIA RATHER THAN TRUE MULTIPLE PERSONALITIES.
SOME KIND OF SHOCK CAUSED HIS OLD MEMORIES TO BE LOST, WHILE SIMULTANEOUSLY...
BUT YOU SAID HIS PERSONALITY CHANGED.
HIS MOTHER IS THE PROBLEM.
SHE INSISTS THAT HE'S "NOT HER SON," WHICH HAS AN UNDERSTANDABLY POWERFUL EFFECT ON THE BOY.

HE'S REACHING THE LIMITS OF HIS ABILITY TO NAVIGATE THIS TENSION.

I DOUBT HE CAN MAINTAIN HIS SENSE OF SELF, LIVING LIKE THAT...

DR. KATSUKO!!
...
THAT'S...
THAT'S ...
THANK YOU VERY MUCH...
...IMPOSSIBLE...
RITSUKA ...
THIS MAY BE HARD FOR YOU TO UNDER-STAND.
BUT IT'S OKAY FOR PEOPLE TO LIVE THEIR LIVES FOR THEMSELVES.
I CAN'T. MY CURFEW IS SIX.
Crud.
I wanna go!
I wanna go...
...on a date.
Yeah, too bad.
AH WELL. TOO BAD... I SUPPOSE.
YOU KNOW, I LIKE YOU THE WAY YOU ARE NOW.
BUT MY MOTHER DOESN'T.
YEAH !
LET'S DO IT!!
YAY !!
TA-DA!
DOCTOR! WILL YOU TAKE A PICTURE WITH ME ?
IT'S NOT LIKE I THINK IT'S A BAD THING.

IT'S NOT LIKE I THINK THAT "BEING MYSELF" IS A BAD THING, REALLY...

BUT...

...IS A SIN.
HOW WAS IT? IS THE THERAPY WORKING?
BBDMP
BBDMP
I'M THE ONLY ONE WHO DOESN'T REMEMBER "RITSUKA."
I'M SORRY.
SO RITSUKA.
YOU'VE COME BACK TO ME, HAVEN'T YOU?
RITSUKA?
I'M STILL ...
...NOT ...
...SO I CAN'T EVEN PRETEND.
!!
...
SHAKE
SHAKE...

HOW COULD I EVER LEAVE MY MOTHER WHEN SHE'S SO SAD?
BUT DR. KATSUKO, HOW CAN I DO THAT?
"IT'S OKAY TO LIVE YOUR LIFE FOR YOURSELF."
NGH...
WHY...?
WHERE DID RITSUKA GO?
SOB
RITSUKA...
SOB
NGH...!
HOW AM I SUPPOSED TO LIVE FOR MYSELF?
CHOMP
HHCK!
I DON'T GET IT, DR. KATSUKO.

WHO ARE YOU? YOU'RE NOT RITSUKA!
GIVE ME BACK MY RITSUKA!!
...
She bit me.
Wasn't on my guard.
STING
STING
WHAT ARE YOU DOING HERE?!
WHAP
MISAKI!
WHY DO YOU HAVE RITSUKA'S FACE?! YOU'RE NOT HIM!!
!
GIVE HIM BACK TO ME!
GRAB
STOP IT, MISAKI!
RITSUKA'S SICK!
I'M BEGGING YOU!! GIVE HIM BACK!
GET OUT OF HERE!
IT'S OKAY.
IF SHE WANTS TO BITE ME, SHE CAN BITE ME.
SHE CAN HIT ME AND CURSE AT ME.
STING
I'm bleeding.
She'll break a tooth.
AFTER ALL...

THIS IS A SIN FOR WHICH I DESERVE TO BE PUNISHED.

BONG
BING
SO...
TODAY ...
AFTER YOU DRAW A PICTURE OF A FRIEND ...
... WE'LL ALL TALK ABOUT FRIEND-SHIP.
MURMUR
MURMUR
RITSUKA !
R-RITSUKA.
WHAT ARE YOU READING ?
HMM ?
GRRR
N4-479-79064-0
95 ¥1600E
from Freud's psychiatry...
there can be a misunderstanding relati
compared
thinkers there's an
each pers
obliterate

Papers: Starry Sky; student name

THEN YOU FORGIVE YUIKO?!
UH...
No...
I'm the one apologizing.
...
SURE.
Do you listen at all?
Oh, forget it.
HEH HEH.
HEH HEH...
HEH HEH HEH ...
She's so weird.
SO WHAT ARE YOU READING?
AN INTRO TO NIETZSCHE.
HUH?
HE TALKED ABOUT HOW "GOD IS DEAD," AND HE DIED OF VENEREAL DISEASE.
...SO IT'S INTERESTING?
YEAH, DO YOU WANT TO BORROW IT?
YUIKO DOESN'T READ.
She's literate !!
BUT Y'KNOW ...
Tee hee!
YUIKO'S ASKING BECAUSE YUIKO WANTS TO KNOW!
...
THAT'S OKAY, ISN'T IT?
YEAH, THAT'S GOOD.
I DON'T LIKE PEOPLE WHO JUST BLINDLY OBEY.

CHATTER
OKAY!
EVERY-ONE FIND A BUDDY.
CHATTER
WHO-EVER YOU LIKE.
HUH?
WHAT ABOUT YUIKO ?
WE'RE ALREADY PAIRED OFF.
DEAL WITH IT.
HUH?
EH?
HUH ?
IDIOT.
Oh boy.
YOU ALREADY HAVE SOMEBODY ELSE TO PAIR WITH, YUIKO.
RIGHT.
RIGHT.
RIGHT.
HUH?
YUIKO'S THE ODD ONE OUT?
REALLY ?
EH?
HUH?
What a cliché.
Exiled from the girls.
WAFFLE WAFFLE WAFFLE
My head hurts.

LOOK!
I'M SAYING I'LL PAIR UP WITH YOU.
?
RITSUKA ...
You awake?
SCOOT
OH!
THANKS!
HEY!
Sigh. Man...
WHO'S GONNA DRAW FIRST?
SHA
SHA
I can't watch.
DON'T GET INVOLVED WITH ME.
THEY'LL JUST LEAVE YOU OUT AGAIN.
It's too dumb.
HUH?
BUT YOU'RE ALWAYS SUPPOSED TO BE NICE TO A NEW STUDENT.

WELL, LOOK.
YOU'RE NOT A COMPLETE IDIOT AFTER ALL.
THAT'S WHAT YUIKO THINKS ANYWAY.
...
YOU TWO! QUIET DOWN, PLEASE!
HEY!
DON'T LOOK!
WAH
WAH!
WHAT'S WITH-OH.
WOW, RITSUKA. YOU SUCK AT ART.
NO WAY.
HMPH!
IT'S NOT "LOOK"! IT'S YUIKO!!
SAY YUIKO!
HOW COME ?!
BEAM
BEAM
BEAM
MRRRGH...
MS. SHINONOME, HOW IS YOUR NEW STUDENT DOING?

QUITE WELL, THANKS!
WHAT...?
OF COURSE NOT.
HE SEEMS TO BE ADJUSTING.
NO BEHAVIOR PROBLEMS?
HE'S A LITTLE SHORT WITH PEOPLE, BUT ASIDE FROM THAT...
IT'S JUST THAT HE'S BEEN THROUGH SOMETHING AWFUL, SO...
SAY...
...WHAT?
PEEK
YOU DIDN'T HEAR ABOUT THE INCIDENT? RITSUKA AOYAGI'S OLDER BROTHER WAS KILLED.
WHAT... RITSUKA'S BROTHER?
...!
Yaiju Junior Elementary School

SOUBI ...!!
Don't follow me.
No, Yuiko wants to walk home together!
Let's hang out!
You don't have cram school, right?
Let's play!
RITSUKA.
I MISSED YOU.
RITSUKA !
...
...
Not that ... again.
I WAS GOING TO GIVE THIS TO YOU THE NEXT TIME WE MET.
SHUFF
WHOA.
It's an adult!
WOW !
WHOA ...

HERE.
All so.
OH... THE PHOTOS.
YOU PRINTED THEM OUT. THANKS.
THAT'S VERY NICE.
I'LL CHERISH THEM.
RITSUKA ?
WHO'S HE?
...
WHO'S THIS GUY?
HEY HEY!
TODAY ...
LIKE BEFORE ...
THIS IS A PROB-LEM.
...RITSUKA HAS THAT DANGEROUS LOOK ON HIS FACE.
IT'S GOT NOTHING TO DO WITH YOU.
HEY, NO FAIR!
WHAT IS IT THAT YOU'RE SEARCHING FOR?
IF YOU DON'T LEARN TO CONCEAL THAT LOOK...
...THAT UNDIS-GUISED YEARNING ...
...SOMEONE WILL SURELY STEAL YOU AWAY.

R...
THEN COME WITH ME.
RITSUKA !!
I WANT YOU TO EXPLAIN WHAT ALL THAT STUFF YESTERDAY WAS ABOUT.
NEVER TOO BUSY FOR YOU.
ARE YOU...
...BUSY NOW?
WHAT THE HECK ?!
...startled You... me.
Whoa.
LET'S ALL GO TO YUIKO'S HOUSE! NOBODY'S HOME.
DON'T LEAVE YUIKO OUT!
PLEASE!
...ALL GO?
THEN SHALL WE...
LET'S GO! LET'S GO!
RITSUKA !
OKAY! ALL RIGHT!
FOOMP
YUIKO'S A LATCHKEY KID!

OHH!
A CONVENIENCE STORE!
7 ELEVEN
コンビニエンス
銀行ATM
LET'S GO IN!
THERE'S NOTHING TO EAT AT HOME.
SURE.
HOLD ON A MINUTE!
YOU'RE NOT GOING TO EAT CONVENIENCE STORE FOOD, ARE YOU?
BUT YUIKO LIKES THEIR BURRITOS.
I LIKE IT TOO.
AND CHEESECAKE AND PUDDING.
RICE BALLS AND BENTO LUNCHES.
THAT'S NO GOOD ...
...FOR GROWING BODIES.
HOW COME ?
WHAT DO YOU MEAN NO GOOD ...?
Tastes good.
I'LL MAKE SOMETHING WITH WHATEVER YOU HAVE AT YOUR HOUSE, YUIKO.

WELL THEN...
YUIKO'S NOT SUPPOSED TO USE THE KITCHEN WHEN YUIKO'S HOME ALONE.
OR TURN THE GAS ON AND STUFF.
I'M SOUBI AGATSUMA.
UH, HE'S SOUBI...
WHO IS HE ?
HMM... WHAT HAVE WE HERE? BURDOCK AND CHICKEN...
TUNK
BEFORE YOU FUSS ABOUT THE KITCHEN...
YOU'RE AWFULLY PICKY.
WE JUST HAVE TO MAKE SURE WE DON'T LEAVE ANY EVIDENCE.
WHAT ?!
DON'T TEACH HER TO BE BAD!
NO WAY I'M EATING BURDOCK, OKAY?
WHAT DO YOU LIKE, THEN?
...MAYBE YOU SHOULDN'T LET STRANGERS IN THE HOUSE?
YOU'RE SUPPOSED TO BE AN ADULT!
IT'S BAD?

MCDONALD'S.
UGH...
THAT'S FINE... EVERY NOW AND THEN.
YOU HAVE TO EAT RIGHT.
I'm borrowing this apron.
YOU NEED TO TRAIN ALL FIVE SENSES.
WHAT FIVE SENSES?
SIGHT, HEARING, SMELL, TOUCH AND TASTE.
WHY THE FIVE SENSES?
PEOPLE USUALLY JUST SAY JUNK FOOD'S BAD FOR YOUR HEALTH.
THE FIVE SENSES...
...RELY ON ORGANS THAT CAN BE TRAINED TO BE SENSITIVE.
FIRST YOU NEED TO TRAIN THE SENSORY ORGANS.
EYES, EARS, NOSE, SKIN, AND TONGUE.
EATING STIMULATES YOUR TASTE BUDS OF COURSE, AS WELL AS YOUR NOSE AND THE NERVE ENDINGS IN YOUR TONGUE.
AND THE TONGUE IS VERY SENSITIVE, WHICH IS WHY IT HURTS WHEN BITTEN.

SHFF
HERE WE GO.
CHICKEN AND SHAVED BURDOCK SPAGHETTI.
HUH?!
SMELLS AWE-SOME!
AND IT LOOKS DELI-CIOUS.
THAT'S GROSS.
WHO'S GONNA BITE A TONGUE? NOT ME.
YOU THINK SO?
IF YOU ASK ME, I'D SAY IT FEELS NICE.
RITSUKA!
SOUBI!
SEE YOU TO-MOR-ROW!!
KAW
ARE YOU COLD?
I'LL WALK YOU HOME.
NOPE.
Again
Tomorrow?
Ugh.
WAVE
KAW

...GOING TO EXPLAIN ABOUT THE OTHER DAY?
SO ARE YOU...
THE ONLY ONE WHO CAN FIGHT AGAINST THE ONES WHO KILLED SEIME!...
...IS ME.
YOU WANT TO KILL THE ENEMY, RIGHT?
I LOVE YOU, RITSUKA.

HOW CAN HE TALK ABOUT MURDER...
...AND LOVE...
...IN THE SAME BREATH?
I KNEW IN MY GUT...
SO YOU KNOW?
YOU KNOW WHO KILLED SEIMEI?!
WHAT DO YOU KNOW?
WHO DID IT...?
DID YOU LOOK FOR SEIMEI'S WILL?
...
HE WASN'T LYING.
HIS WILL?
I NEVER THOUGHT...
WHERE WOULD HIS WILL BE?!
I DIDN'T KNOW ADULTS COULD BE LIKE THIS.
ONLY A SPELL BATTLE, FOUGHT WITH WORDS, WILL WORK AGAINST THIS ENEMY.
HE'S SO STRANGE!
WE FIGHT IN PAIRS. I AM THE FIGHTER.

YOU ARE THE SACRIFICE, RITSUKA.
DURING BATTLE, THE SACRIFICE BEARS THE DAMAGE INFLICTED UPON THE FIGHTER.
"SACRIFICE"? LIKE AN OFFERING!
IF THE SACRIFICE GETS WORN DOWN, YOU LOSE.
BUMP
IT IS VERY ...
...VERY PAINFUL.
YOU WILL SUFFER. CAN YOU HANDLE IT?
BUMP
BUMP
CAN YOU HANDLE UNBEARABLE SUFFERING, RITSUKA?
OF COURSE.
BUMP
I CAN DO IT!

SEIMEI'S WILL.
TMP TMP
RITSUKA.
WHERE COULD IT BE ?
WHAT IS IT?
WHAT'S THE MATTER, RITSUKA ?
PLEASE COME OUT.
BAM BAM BAM
YOU LIKE CHESTNUT RICE, DON'T YOU?
I MADE YOUR FAVORITE DISHES.
ZWEEEE
I HAVEN'T TURNED IT ON SINCE SEIMEI DIED.
IT'S OKAY, MOM.
RITSUKA!
BAM BAM BAM
I'LL BE THERE SOON.
BAM
THE COMPUTER !!
LATER.
IT'S JUST... I'M SORRY, MOM.
BAM BAM BAM
JUST WAIT.
NO.
GET OUT HERE, RITSUKA!
RITSUKA !

HUH?
TAK TAK
GOOD EVENING.
...
THIS IS THE SECOND FLOOR.
CHAK
AND? I'M HERE.
WHATEVER YOU WANT. I'LL DO WHATEVER YOU LIKE.
SHE'S MAKING A FUSS. SHALL I SILENCE HER?
BAM BAM
THAT'S MY MOTHER.
SHE'S MY MOTHER AND SEIMEI'S TOO. DON'T DO ANY-THING.
JUST LEAVE HER ALONE.
BAM
IS THIS IT?
TAK
TAK
TAK
RITSUKA
ARGH ...
THE ENTIRE FOLDER IS LOCKED.
WHAT'S THE PASSWORD ?

BWOOP
DAMN.
INPUT FAILED. TRY AGAIN?
CANCEL
THAT'S NOT IT.
HOW ABOUT ...
...
MAYBE "BELOVED" ...?
PASS-WORD ...
TAK TAK
PLEASE ENTER YOUR ID AND PASSWORD.
ID:
RITSUKA
PASSWORD:
HEY...
GULP
WHAT DID YOU CALL ME?
CHK
YOUR REAL NAME, RITSUKA, IS...
LOVELESS.
英数
WHO DECIDED THAT?!
WHAT'S THE DEAL WITH THAT?
THAT'S HORRIBLE ...
IT MEANS "WITHOUT LOVE."

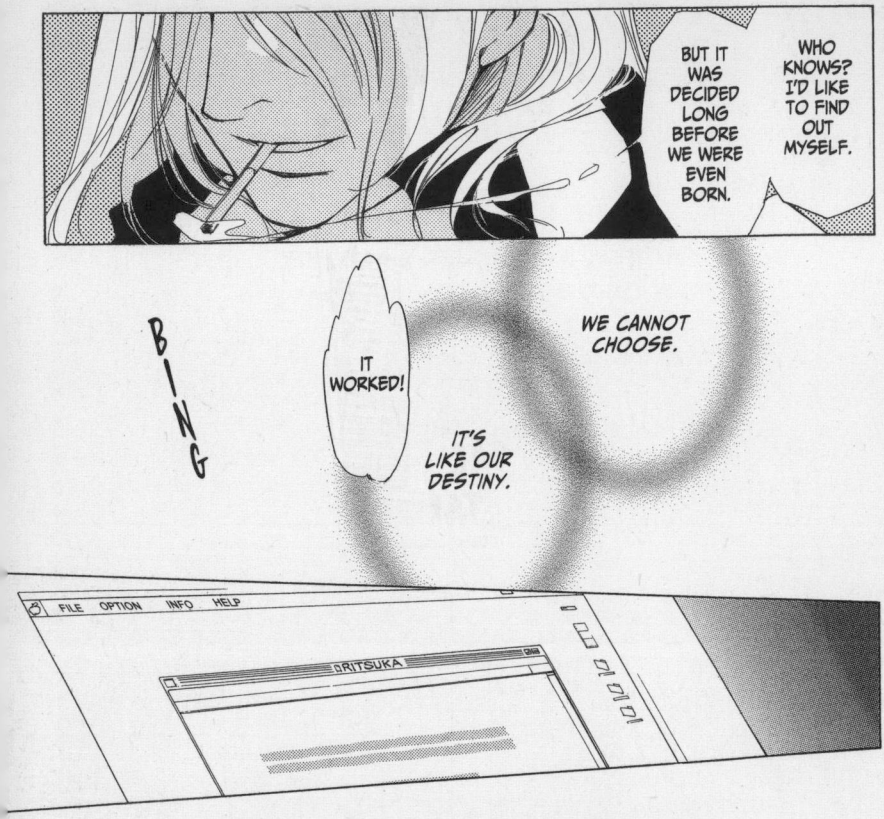

If I am dead, it means I was murdered.
This is information on my murderer.

RITSUKA

Hey, there.
I figure that if I die, you'll eventually find this.
If I am dead, it means I was murdered.
This is information on my murderer.

(I trust that you'll find this)

I will be killed by Septimal Moon.

To Ritsuka.
I leave you a Fighter.

WHAT IS THE MEANING OF THIS, SOUBI?
WHAT IS THIS?!
FWIP
YOU'RE HERE BECAUSE SEIMEI TOLD YOU TO FIND ME?
THAT'S RIGHT.
YOU SAID...
YOU SAID YOU LOVED ME!!
OVER AND OVER!
WHY?
JUST BECAUSE SEIMEI TOLD YOU TO?!
RITSUKA'S VOICE IS ELECTRIFYING.
ANSWER ME!
SOUBI!!
IT'S THE VOICE...
...OF THE ONE WHO WILL COMMAND ME.

YES.
DID SEIMEI ...
...TELL YOU TO LOVE ME?
HE DID.
SO YOU JUST DO WHATEVER SEIMEI SAYS.
YOU'RE FINE WITH THAT?
I AM.
SEIMEI'S WORD IS ABSOLUTE.
AND NOW I'VE BEEN TOLD TO OBEY RITSUKA'S COMMANDS.
YOU CAN'T LOVE SOMEONE...
...BECAUSE YOU WERE COMMANDED TO.
THAT'S NOT RIGHT...!!
BUT I LOVE YOU.
SHUT UP!
I DON'T WANT TO HEAR IT!!

THERE'S NO USE CRYING ABOUT IT.
BUT YOU'RE STILL GOING TO NEED ME.
ONLY I CAN FIGHT FOR YOU.
I'M NOT...
...CRYING !!
THERE'S NOTHING!! THERE'S NOTHING THAT BELONGS TO ME! NOT SEIMEI OR SOUBI OR MOM! NOTHING...!

WHAT ABOUT ME?
WHAT AM I EVEN DOING HERE?
EVERYTHING BELONGS TO "RITSUKA."
KRUU
"RITSUKA."
ANYWAY! SEPTIMAL MOON!
I'LL NEVER FORGIVE WHOEVER KILLED SEIMEI. WHAT DID SEIMEI EVER DO TO DESERVE SOMETHING LIKE THAT?!

CHIRP
MURMUR
MURMUR
IT'S TRUE, I SWEAR!
I HEARD THE TEACHERS TALKING ABOUT IT.
MURMUR
SEE HERE?
THE VICTIM WAS SEIMEI AOYAGI, AGE 17.
TRAGED
THE SHOCKED CLASSROOM!!
THAT'S AOYAGI'S OLDER BROTHER.
"HE WAS SET ON FIRE WHILE STILL ALIVE."
"AND AFTERWARDS, THE BODY WAS RE-CLOTHED AND LEFT IN AN ELEMENTARY SCHOOL CLASSROOM."
"THE CULPRIT HAS NOT YET BEEN FOUND."
FREAKY!
THAT'S SICK... WHAT A PERVERT!
HEY... KNOCK IT OFF!!
MURMUR
WHAT'S THIS GOT TO DO WITH RITSUKA?
COME ON, THIS IS GOOD STUFF!
LIKE, THIS GUY WAS A HIGH SCHOOLER, SO WHY DID HE DIE IN AN ELEMENTARY SCHOOL?
STOP IT!!
IT'S GONNA MAKE RITSUKA UPSET IF HE HEARS!

I'M GOING TO KILL THEM TOO.
GASP
YOU KNOW ...
...THEY LEFT HIM IN MY SEAT.
MY BROTHER'S CORPSE.
I'M PRETTY CURIOUS MYSELF, YOU KNOW.
ABOUT WHO KILLED MY BROTHER.
IF YOU GET TOO CLOSE TO ME...
...YOU MIGHT GET KILLED, BURNED AND LEFT IN MY CHAIR TOO.
WAAAH
!!
EW, GROSS !!

TMP TMP
RITSUKA! UH...
YUIKO'S REALLY SORRY!
WAIT!
TMP TMP TMP
RITSUKA!
GRAB
LOOK, SHUT UP! DON'T APOLOGIZE.
IT'S NOT YOUR BUSINESS!
LET GO!
TUG
BUT... YUIKO FEELS BAD!
LET HER MAKE IT UP TO YOU!
DON'T BOTHER ME! LET GO!
NO!
NO...
NO...
YUIKO...
SOB...
...WANTS TO BE...
...FRIENDS WITH YOU, RITSUKA...
I'M...
JUST...
WHATEVER. I DON'T NEED ANYBODY.
I'M TIRED.

IT DOESN'T MATTER IF I LAUGH OR CRY ANYMORE.
SO WHY SMILE ?
IT JUST WEARS ME OUT!
SORRY RITSUKA. YUIKO DOESN'T GET IT...
BUT... YOU SOUND LONELY.
HUG
YUIKO HATES BEING LONELY!!
YUIKO DOESN'T WANT YOU TO BE LONELY, RITSUKA!
NGH ...
YUIKO'S HERE FOR YOU!
YUIKO'S HERE FOR YOU.
YUIKO WILL BE YOUR FRIEND... SO PLEASE !!
DON'T CRY.

YO!
LOVE-LESS.
FLINCH
WHERE'S SOUBI? HE'S NOT HERE?
YOU ...!
...
HUH? WHAT HOME-ROOM ARE THEY FROM?
WE'RE HERE TO COLLECT YOU.
BY ORDER OF SEPTIMAL MOON.
GASP
SEPTIMAL MOON...?
YOU TWO!

YUIKO!
I'LL MAKE IT UP TO YOU LATER, SO JUST DO IT.
BUT... RITSUKA ?
IT'S FINE, JUST HURRY. GO BACK.
BUT...
CALL SOUBI.
YOU AREN'T GONNA COME QUIETLY, ARE YOU?
WHAT...
WHAT'S GOING ON?
GO BACK TO THE CLASS-ROOM.
BLUSH
NO COM-MENT.
WHY DID YOU KILL SEIMEI?
I JUST WANT TO ASK ONE THING.
TMP! TMP! TMP!

CHAPTER 3

C'MON.
YOU'RE COMING BACK WITH US.
AS IF I'D EVER GO WITH THEM!
ABOUT SEIMEI... WHY DID YOU KILL HIM?
HMPH
NO COM-MENT.
GRR!
!
GLANCE

YOU DIDN'T DENY IT.
YOU REALLY... MURDERED HIM?
IT'S NOT LIKE I DID IT PERSONALLY.
SEPTIMAL MOON KILLED HIM.
WHAT IS SEPTIMAL MOON?
NO COMMENT!
WHY ARE YOU HARASSING ME?
NO COMMENT!
C'MON, IT DOESN'T MATTER. JUST DO AS YOU'RE TOLD!
PLEASE. LIKE I'M GOING TO LISTEN TO YOU.
FEEH
WHY BOTHER ASKING?
FIGURES.
BUT IT'S ALREADY BEEN DECIDED THAT YOU'RE COMING TO SEPTIMAL MOON.
WHAT YOU WANT HAS NOTHING TO DO WITH IT.
NOK NOK

DID I KEEP YOU WAITING...
RITSUKA ?
SOUBI.
WHAT DO I DO...?
YOU SAID THAT YOU'D FIGHT FOR ME, RIGHT?
BLUSH
OF COURSE. WE'LL FIGHT.
CLAK
JUST TRUST ME.
CLAK
I WANT TO BELIEVE HIM.

LET US BATTLE.
AGREED!!
VWEEN
VWEEN

SYSTEMS EXPAND.
WEEN
OVER AND OVER !!
DESTROY !!
DEFEND !!
DOH
DEFEND !!
THAT WITHOUT SHAPE SHALL PROTECT THIS BODY.
BWOO
NO POWER CAN REACH ME.
SHAA

RE-VERSE!
RE-FLECT!
RE-PULSE!
!!
POWER DIS-CHARGED ...
...SHALL RETURN TO THE SOURCE.
HE'S FAST!
VIP
DEFEND !!
DEFEND !!
DEFEND !
VIP
AGH!
HE DEFLECT-ED IT!
VIP
CALM DOWN, AI.
THAT WON'T WORK.
MI-DORI !
JUST REPEATING THE SAME WORD IS INEFFECTIVE.
DO YOU EVEN KNOW WHAT YOU'RE DOING?

CHANG
AGH!!
SHWAAA
RIP !!
BLAST !!
FWOO
PSHA
PSHA
PSHA
!!!
WH...
WHAT'S THAT ?
THAT'S A RESTRICTION.
RESTRICTION
IT'S THE DAMAGE THAT A SACRIFICE RECEIVES.

MIDORI!
THIS IS NOTHING! KEEP GOING!
IT'S MORE IMPORTANT FOR YOU TO REACT PROPERLY.
HE'S CHOOSING HIS WORDS QUICKLY AND PRECISELY.
AND HE'S LINKING THEM TOGETHER.
YOU WON'T BE ABLE TO ATTACK IF YOU'RE BUSY DEFENDING ME.
IF YOU RESTRICT THAT SACRIFICE...
...YOU CAN INFLICT FOUR TIMES THE NORMAL AMOUNT OF DAMAGE.
AFTER ALL, THEIR NAMES ARE DIFFERENT.
TRY CUTTING.
FWOO
GOT IT.
C..
CUT APART.
SEVER.
KREEE
ROTATE.
DIVERT THE BODY'S COURSE OF ORBIT!
DIF-FRACT.
CUT APART THE BODY.
WHETHER A LITTLE SLICE OR A BIG GASH...
I'LL CUT THEM APART!
FWOO

BZZRT
NGH...
I DID IT!
!!
CHANG
SHANK
CHANG
CHANG
CUT AGAIN!
CUT APART!
FWOOVWEEE
THAT ATTACK IS FUTILE. EVADE AND RE-CUPER-ATE.
ONCE MORE, ROTATE AND DIFFRACT.
IN-SCRIBE AN ORBIT.
NGH...
I DIDN'T DODGE WELL ENOUGH?

HUFF ...
AH ...
It's tight.
DOES IT HURT, RITSUKA ?
THIS ...
DID SEIMEI... DO THIS TOO?
THAT'S RIGHT.
CUT...
YOU'RE SO BRAVE.
OW.
CLINK
THEN I CAN HANDLE IT!
DENY !!
NGH!

NGH ...
DEFEND !
FULL POWER ...!!
I SHALL INFLUENCE AND INVADE YOU.
I SHALL INFILTRATE AND IMPEDE YOUR ESCAPE. I SHALL SWALLOW YOUR FREEDOM AND LOCK YOU DOWN.
STOP.
SUS-PEND.
INTER-FERE.
INTER-VENE.
FAIL.
DEFENSE FAILS.
ALL WALLS WILL CRUMBLE.
FWOO
AGH!!
BSH
BSH
RITSUKA.
KISS ME.
CLANK

HUH ...
WHA ...?!
WHOA!
NO WAY !!
ZSH
WHAT ?!
CHANG
NGH ...
FALL TO CHAOS ...
LITTLE BRATS WITH YOUR LITTLE EARS!
I KNOW THINGS THAT YOU DON'T KNOW.
ANNIHILATE !!
DEFEAT

...
YOU SAID YOU WERE GOING TO KILL THEM.
BUT IT'S FINE. I'LL DO WHATEVER YOU LIKE.
GULP
...!!
WHAT ARE YOU GOING TO DO WITH THEM ...?
THOSE GUYS ARE SEPTIMAL MOON!
WHAT DO YOU WANT ME TO DO? KILL THEM?
RIT-SUKA?
YOU OKAY?
JOLT
NO...
I'M NOT GOING TO KILL PEOPLE.
GRIT
...

THEN I'M GOING TO GO RETURN THEM.
THERE'S A GOOD BOY.
I WON'T KILL...!
I LOVE YOU ... RITSUKA.
I DON'T...
I DON'T WANT TO HEAR IT!!
JUST GO AWAY !!
SKWEE
SEE YOU.
HOW CAN YOU SAY "I LOVE YOU" ...?

SOUBI.

I HEAR THOSE WORDS AND YOU KISS ME...

...AND I START TO BELIEVE YOU.

I've had... enough!

NGH...

NGH...

WHY ARE YOU...?

WHAT AM I SUPPOSED TO DO?

WHY DID YOU HAVE TO COME HERE AND TURN ME ALL UPSIDE DOWN?

I'LL KEEP MY PROMISE.
DO YOU STILL WANT TO BE FRIENDS?
My head hurts.
REALLY ?! YUIKO CAN ?!
YEAH.
F...
FOR SURE!
YES !!
FLICK
THEN...
TRMBL
FROM NOW ON, STOP CALLING YOURSELF YUIKO.
IT'S "I."
TRY IT.
OKAY!
I.
I!!

YUIKO LIKES... I MEAN, I...
BLUSH
THAT'S IT.
I LIKE IT... THAT'S BETTER.
I LOVE IT SO MUCH.
I LOVE RITSUKA'S SMILE.
Exactly.
Got it! So I need to read, right?
Read more books! Read! I thought you were illiterate!
whaaaat?
I hate idiots.
Like you.
And also, you need to get smarter.
HAWA-TARI...
LET'S GO.
OKAY!!

I DON'T THINK ANYONE IN CLASS HAS EVER DONE THIS.
HOW DOES THAT MAKE YOU FEEL?
DON'T YOU FEEL CLEVER?
OR...
...
DO YOU FEEL DIRTY?

BELOVED
YUN KOUGA
...
YOU'RE...
...SURPRISINGLY CHILDISH.
Hmph!
Idiot.

CHAPTER 4

RITSUKA.SOUBI SEIMEI
LOVELESS.....NO_00

PING!

RITSUKA AOYAGI?
WHO'S THAT?
HE SHOWED UP WHILE YOU WERE OUT, YAYOI.
HE'S A TRANSFER STUDENT.
NOD NOD NOD
...
A TRANSFER STUDENT ...
I'M NOT INTER-ESTED.
BUT THIS GUY...
TO YUIKO...?!
WHAT?
...IS REALLY CLOSE TO HAWATARI.

RITSUKA!!
FWIP!!
HOW...
...IS THAT...
YU...
YOU ALWAYS LOOK SO COOL.
WOW!
GOOD MORNING!
HE'S ACTING SO FRIENDLY WITH HER.
YOU READ THAT BOOK I TOLD YOU ABOUT YESTERDAY?
MORNING, YUIKO.
Man, you're loud.
UH HUH!
I SURE DID!
?!?
"COOL"...!

...SHRIMP!
HE'S TOTALLY SHORT!!
BUT...
HE'S A...
KRNCH
WELL, EXCUSE ME FOR BEING SHORT.
BUT...
HMPH
Y...
YAYOI ?
I ♡ BDMP
Shrimp ?
Me?
is that me?

SHOCK
YOU'RE A SHRIMP YOURSELF.
THE ISSUE HERE IS THAT YOU'RE SHORT.
MY HEIGHT IS IRRELEVANT.
I DON'T GET WHAT YOUR PROBLEM IS.
WHAT'S IT TO YOU WHETHER I'M SHORT OR MY TAIL'S LONG OR IF MY EARS ARE COOL-LOOKING?
Two times?
He said it twice?!
KACHING

WAIT! WAIT!
YAYO!!
SHORT PEOPLE AREN'T QUALIFIED!
HUH?!
TO GO OUT WITH YUIKO!
THE ONLY PEOPLE WHO HAVE PERMISSION TO DATE HER...
AAUGH!
...ARE GUYS WHO ARE TALLER THAN SHE IS!
WHO CARES ABOUT THAT?
BLUNT
!!!
...
IT'S NOT LIKE WE'RE DATING.
WE'RE JUST FRIENDS.
RIGHT, YUIKO?
...
...
UH-HUH.
SHRUG
!!
!!
!!

YUIKO ...!!
YOU'RE...
NO...
NO WAY! NO W(AY! NO WAY!
YUIKO CAN'T!!
PANIC
NO!
SHAKE
WHOA
YUIKO!
CALM DOWN!
BLUSH
UH...
YAYOI ?!
WITH YUIKO?!
FWOO
YUIKO.
WILL YOU GO OUT WITH ME?

SNIFF...
YUIKO LIKES YOU, YAYOI. WE'RE FRIENDS AND STUFF...
BUT YUIKO'S ONLY IN SIXTH GRADE.
BLUSH
UH...
IS IT...
FIVE TIMES...
...BECAUSE YOU DON'T LIKE ME...?
SHE SAID NO FIVE TIMES...
WAAAH
SORRY!
UH...
UM...
OKAY?
SHOCK
D-DID I JUMP THE GUN...?
MONDA'S BEEN DATING SINCE FOURTH GRADE. SUZUKI TOO...
ONLY IN SIXTH GRADE...? MIDDLE SCHOOLERS DATE!
SHOCK
OH NO, I MADE HER CRY!
IT'S OKAY, YUIKO.
I'M THE ONE WHO SHOULD BE APOLOGIZING.
SORRY!
YAYOI...
ACK...

CRACK
YUIKO CAN'T GO OUT WITH PEOPLE WHO'RE SHORTER THAN HER.
168cm
Thanks.
147cm
BWAAAH
SORRY.
YES! THAT'S IT.
I SEE NOW...
UNGH...
TRMBL
THAT...
I...
WHA...
OH...
TRMBL
WHAT'S...
...WHO WANTS TO CRY.
TRMBL
I'M THE ONE...
TRMBL
TRMBL
!!
LET'S GO, YUIKO.
WE'RE GOING TO BE LATE.

WHO THE HELL WAS THAT GUY? HE WAS WEIRD...
SEE THAT?
HOW IS THAT NOT DATING?!
THAT'S WHAT AOYAGI SAYS...
...CONTRARY TO THE EVIDENCE.
I...
I'M SORRY, RITSUKA.
WHY ARE YOU APOLOGIZING, YUIKO?
SOR ...
BESIDES, HEIGHT DOESN'T MATTER. THAT'S STUPID.
SOR ...
~~Yuiko~~ I mean, I...
WHO DOES THAT YAYOI THINK HE IS?
HE'S GOT A GIRLY NAME.
STRUT
STRUT

RITSUKA AOYAGI. SIXTH GRADE, CLASS 3.
HE'S CUTE, ISN'T HE?
LIKE A GIRL.
ANYWAY, I FIGURE I'M GOING TO GROW SOON...
...AND GET A LOT TALLER.
AFTER ALL, SEIMEI WAS TALL.

OKAY.
I'M HANDING BACK YOUR MATH TESTS.
THE TOP SCORE WAS 100! RITSUKA AOYAGI!!
UDA-GAWA!
Here!
ANDO!
ITO!
YAY
YAY
BUT EVERYONE DID PRETTY WELL THIS TIME.
I'M REALLY PROUD OF YOU! ♡
WELL, THERE'S ONLY ONE POSSIBLE ANSWER IN MATH.
YOU SHOULD GET A PERFECT SCORE TOO, YUIKO.
Make Ms. Shinoname happy.
RITSUKA, THAT'S GREAT! ♡
YOU GOT A PERFECT SCORE! ♡

DON'T SAY THINGS ARE IMPOSSIBLE.
I HATE THAT WORD.
WHAAA?!
NO WAY.
THAT'S IMPOSSIBLE.
DON'T TALK LIKE THAT.
DUMMY.
OKAY!
TOMORROW IS SATURDAY, BUT IT'S PARENTS' DAY.
ENCOURAGE YOUR FATHER TO COME!
BOW!
GOODBYE!
BING BONG
OKAY, THAT'S ALL FOR TODAY.
CLEANING TIME!
SKRUT
SKRUT
SKRUT
ATTENTION!
CHATTER
CHATTER
Yeah.
Library time?
RITSUKA.
CAN I HAVE A WORD WITH YOU?

YOU SEE...
RITSUKA, IT'S JUST...
THERE HASN'T BEEN A SIGNATURE SHOWING THAT YOUR PARENTS HAVE SEEN YOUR SCHOOL-WORK. THE "I'VE READ IT" CONFIRMATION?
SO I WAS WONDERING WHAT WAS GOING ON...?
Oh...
That...
...
YES.
YUIKO, GO AHEAD TO THE LIBRARY.
HUUUH?
OH.
SOUBI!
I SEE YOU!
HI!
HIYA
OH...!
BEEEEE!!
SOW...!
BDMP
SOU...

SOUBI...
...IS HERE!!
I WANT TO SEE HIM...
AFTER ALL, EVEN IF I SEE HIM...
I DON'T WANT TO SEE HIM...
SOUBI'S HERE TO PICK YOU UP.
I'M GONNA WAIT WITH HIM!
HEY...
YUIKO.
TMP TMP
HE ISN'T HERE TO PICK US UP.
HE JUST CAME BECAUSE HE FELT LIKE IT...

SELFISH SOUBI...
BECAUSE HE FELT LIKE IT...
...HE'S JUST GOING TO MESS ME UP AGAIN.
IF I SEE HIM...
...IT HURTS TO SEE HIM...
...BUT...
I WANT TO SEE HIM...

HE WAS A FRIEND OF MY DEAD BROTHER.
HIS NAME IS AGATSUMA.
HIM?
OH.

WHO'S THAT...?
RITSUKA ?!

OH...
I SEE...

...HANGS OUT WITH ME SOME-TIMES.
HE...
AND, UH...

RITSUKA, WAIT. YOU NEED TO GET THAT SIGNATURE.
HEY.
DASH
LATER, I'VE GOTTA GO.

SIGNA-TURE?
REALLY ?
I DON'T NEED IT, DO I? I GET GOOD GRADES.
MY PARENTS DON'T SAY ANYTHING ANYWAY.

THAT'S NOT WHAT I MEAN.
YOU NEED TO HAVE THEM SEE IT AND GET IT SIGNED.
THAT'S WEIRD.
FINE, THEN.
IF YOU WANT IT, THEN I'LL HAVE THEM DO IT.
I'll sign...
RITSUKA!!
HEY NOW!
THAT'S THE FIRST TIME I'VE SEEN...
...THAT EXPRESSION ON RITSUKA'S FACE.
HE LOOKED SO CUTE.
I WONDER WHO THIS AGATSUMA IS.

MY BROTHER SEIMEI...

HE ALWAYS TALKED TO ME...
...IN A WAY I COULD UNDERSTAND.
BUT SOUBI...

HE ALWAYS HAS SECRETS... HE'S ALWAYS HIDING THINGS... ALWAYS LYING...

RITSUKA! WHAT'S THE MATTER?
QUITE THE BUMP YOU'VE GOT THERE.
I TOLD YOU TO RUN WHEN MOM STARTS GETTING OUT OF CONTROL, RIGHT?
I'M OKAY.
THIS IS NOTHING.
IT DOESN'T HURT.
JUST RUN.
IF MOM IS ABOUT TO DO SOME-THING TO YOU...
...JUST RUN TO ME.
PLUCK
OKAY?
...
...
OKAY.
BUT NOW...

I HAVE NOWHERE TO RUN.
WHY ARE YOU HERE?!
WHAT THE HELL DO YOU WANT NOW?!
SOUBI!
HUFF
Jerk
Jerk
DAMMIT ...
YOU-!
Jerk
Jerk
HUFF
YOU'RE LATE!
THREE DAYS, I THINK ?
HOW LONG DO YOU THINK IT'S BEEN ?!
THAT'S RIGHT! YOU LEFT ME HANGING FOR THREE WHOLE DAYS!

YOU JERK!
NO!
DON'T USE THAT WORD. I HATE IT.
YOU CAN JUST...
...“DIE”?
Hmm.
YOU CAN JUST...
...“LOVE ME”?
TWITCH
WH...?!
THAT'S NOT IT!!
YOU CAN JUST...!

YES, I'M A COLLEGE STUDENT.
SORRY I COULDN'T COME SEE YOU.
A... STU-DENT?
YOU, SOUBI?
He is?
...didn't know.
WOW!
YOU'RE GOING OUT WITH A COLLEGE STUDENT, RITSUKA!
What?!
Do you hear yourself?
NO. WE'RE NOT DATING.
WE'RE MASTER AND SERVANT.
MUSTARD ... AND ...?
What?
What's that...
...supposed to mean?
SPIN
SPIN
SHFF
I CAME HERE TO CONNECT WITH YOU.
HERE.

MY NUMBER IS THE FIRST ONE IN THE ADDRESS BOOK.
CALL ME ANYTIME.
WHAT'S THIS ...?
WHATEVER. I'M NOT DOING THAT.
AWW. HOW COME? JUST CALL ME.
HERE'S THE CHARGER.
SKWEEZ
I CAN'T... ACCEPT THIS.
I DON'T KNOW WHY YOU'RE DOING THIS.
YOU CAN ALSO SEND ME EMAIL.
YOU KNOW HOW, RIGHT?
HERE.

THERE'S A PERFECTLY GOOD REASON. IT'S SO YOU WON'T BE LONELY, RITSUKA.
SO YOU WON'T GET ANXIOUS.
YOU'LL ALWAYS BE CONNECTED TO ME.

I'M NOT LONELY.
Tel...
Tele-phone.
Phone.
Cell phone.
OH?
THAT'S GREAT, THEN!
PWEEP
PWEEP
PWEEP

HUH?
KIO?
...
YAY!
CAN I PUT MY NUMBER IN YOUR PHONE?

YOU'RE NOT GONNA MAKE IT IN TIME.
IF YOU MISS THE DEADLINE THE PROFESSOR WON'T ACCEPT YOUR WORK.
I'LL BE BACK SOON.
I'M A LITTLE BUSY RIGHT NOW.
YOU'RE FRIGGIN' BUSY?
ISN'T THAT RICH!
HURRY UP AND GET YOUR BUTT BACK HERE.
JEEZ.
AGATSUMA'S SURE GOT IT TOGETHER.
I'M BARELY COMING IN UNDER THE WIRE.
YOU CALL THIS "TOGETHER"?! HE HASN'T FINISHED ANY OF HIS WORK.
WHAT'S THIS "I'M BUSY" CRAP?

AND WHAT'S WITH THIS PICTURE?
IS HE SOME KIND OF PEDO?
WOW, WHAT A CUTIE!
FWIP

OMIGOD, LOOK AT ALL OF THESE!
EEE! HE'S SO CUTE.
AH HA, HE'S GOT HIS EARS!
FWIP
THAT PERVERT !!
CHEATER!

KIO. DON'T GO THROUGH AGATSUMA'S BAG.
HE DOESN'T CARE!!
RUSTL
I'M PRETTY MUCH SOU'S WIFE, ANYWAY!!
UM...
I NEED TO CHECK !

ARGH, I'M CALLING HIM.
THAT PUNK.
HE TURNED HIS PHONE OFF.
DAMN IT. THAT BASTARD!
KIO. COME ON BACK.
AGH!

I WON'T FORGIVE HIM FOR THIS!
NOT WHEN HE HAS SOMEONE LIKE ME!!
GRR
GRR
GRR

YOU'RE A COLLEGE STUDENT...
WHAT ARE YOU...
...STUDYING ?
ART.
JAPANESE ART.
I FOUND OUT FOR THE FIRST TIME TODAY...
JAPA-NESE...
...ART ...?
...?
THAT'S AMAZING.
ONE OF SOUBI'S SECRETS.
YOU THINK SO?
IT IS!! I CAN'T DRAW AT ALL.
RIGHT, YUIKO?!
BDMP
BDMP
BDMP
YUP!
TOTALLY AMAZING !!
BDMP
NEVER ONCE SINCE I MET HIM...
...HAVE I BELIEVED THAT HE REALLY WAS A HUMAN BEING...
...LIKE ME.
THEN NEXT TIME...
...I'LL PAINT A PICTURE FOR YOU, RITSUKA.
SOUBI.

YOU FINALLY SMILED.
I'M GLAD TO SEE YOU'RE IN A BETTER MOOD NOW.
HE PAINTS PICTURES ...
HE GOES TO COLLEGE...
SURE.
REALLY ?
MY SPECIALTY IS FLOWERS.
YAY!
WOW
WHAT ARE YOU GOING TO PAINT?
WOW
WOW
WOW

ALWAYS ...?
YES.
BUT...
CALL ME ANYTIME.
I'LL ALWAYS PICK UP.

I LIVE FOR YOU, RITSUKA.
THERE'S NOTHING I CAN'T DO.
I CAN.
IF IT'S A CALL FROM YOU, I'LL ALWAYS PICK UP.
TRY ME.
YOU CAN'T ALWAYS ANSWER THE PHONE. THAT'S IMPOSSIBLE.
DON'T PROMISE SOMETHING YOU CAN'T DO.
HMM.
OH. REALLY.
...I'LL BET SEIMEI JUST COMMANDED YOU TO DO THAT...RIGHT...?
WHAT ABOUT SOUBI?
I'M SORRY, NOT TODAY.
GO HOME, GET LOST.
I'M GOING HOME TOO.
OH. OKAY.
WE CAN STOP BY A CONVENIENCE STORE.
LET'S GO.
CAN I CALL YOU TOO?
UM! ♡
Aw.
Ritsuka...
...that's cold.
OF COURSE.

BUT...
I'M SORRY.
IT'S ADORABLE.
RITSUKA.
YOU'VE GOT SUCH SLENDER SHOULDERS.
NOW THE TRAINING BEGINS.
...

BRM
RM
6-3
RITSUKA AOYAGI
DAY
TITLE
Bill Gates
Marsha and Dots
Disneyland
WHAT'S WITH THIS LIBRARY CARD?
BOTH SIDES FILLED IN ONLY A WEEK?!
YAYOI!
LET'S GO HOME.
RITSUKA AOYAGI AGAIN?
WAIT A MINUTE.
I'M COMING...

I WONDER IF HE GOT THAT INJURY FROM GYM CLASS.
I GUESS THAT MEANS HE'S IN GOOD SHAPE...
SIGH...
AH. RITSUKA AND I HAVE THAT IN COMMON TOO.
?
夕焼け
六年三組 青柳 立夏
HIS CALLI-GRAPHY ....
...IS REALLY GOOD TOO.
HRM.
Paper: Sunset, Sixth grade Class 3, Ritsuka Aoyagi
KOFF
CRUD.
AH.
UNLIKE...
...ME.
YEAH.
I HAVE MY INHALER, SO I'M OKAY...
GASP
GASP
IT MUST BE THE LOW ATMO-SPHERIC PRESSURE ...
WSH
YAYOI!
YAYOI ...
YOU ALL RIGHT?
KOFF!

IT LOOKS LIKE IT'S ABOUT TO RAIN...
HURTS TO BREATHE.
GASP
GASP
...BUT...
I CAN'T ...
...GIVE UP ON YUIKO ...
...JUST BECAUSE OF HIM.
GASP
PLIP
PLIP
PLIP
AW MAN.
IT'S REALLY COMING DOWN.
THANK YOU VERY MUCH.
CHAK
OH.

GOT IT IN ON TIME, SOU?
SORT OF.
MY PAINTS HAVEN'T DRIED YET...
Ha ha.
CHK
THAT'S WHAT YOU GET FOR SKIPPING OUT, IDIOT.
AND?
"AND" ?
WHO IS HE? THAT KID IN THE PICTURE. IT'S NOT OKAY!
LOOK, KIO.
DON'T GO POKING THROUGH PEOPLE'S BAGS...
GRR
GRRAR
SHUT UP! THAT'S NOT THE ISSUE HERE!
I ASKED YOU A QUESTION, SO ANSWER ME. WHO IS THAT KID?!
THAT BOY...
...IS RITSUKA AOYAGI.
THAT'S ALL I'LL SAY.
GRR
AOYAGI ?!
WHAT ?!

SLUMP
MY HEAD HURTS.
"AOYAGI" ?! THAT'S BAD!
AGH! IT COULDN'T GET ANY WORSE!
HE'S GOT SOMETHING TO DO WITH SEIMEI, RIGHT...?
PEEK
OH MY GOD... HIS KID?
DON'T BE ABSURD.
SEIMEI STILL HAD HIS EARS.
IT'S HIS LITTLE BROTHER.
Oops, I said it.
AGH!
MAN...
THIS SUCKS.
THIS REALLY, REALLY SUCKS.
SOU, YOU'RE GOING TO BECOME ANOTHER AOYAGI'S SLAVE?
JUST WHEN ...
...SEIMEI WAS FINALLY GONE.
KIO.
DON'T SAY THINGS LIKE THAT.
SMH

I DIDN'T MIND.
HE SHACKLED YOU, SOU.
WELL, I DID! I'LL NEVER FORGIVE HIM.
NOPE.
I'M SAYING IT.
I WAS THRILLED WHEN SEIMEI DIED.
KIO!!
...
I'LL BRUTALIZE YOU UNTIL YOU CAN'T STAND IT.
I'M NOT KINKY.
LOOK, SOU, IF YOU'RE INTO THAT KIND OF THING...
...WHY CAN'T IT BE WITH ME?
GOT IT!
IF YOU'RE DONE CLEANING UP, THEN JUST GO HOME ALREADY!
HEY! STOP MAKING ALL THAT RACKET!
KCHAK
WHAT ?! YOU'RE LYING !!

KAIDOU.
WHAT'S UP?
THOSE EARS! IT'S TOO MUCH!
Huh?
BUT THEY'RE COOL, RIGHT?
DON'T ADD ANY MORE. IT'S DISGUSTING.
YES, SIIIIR.
(Empty words.)
CHAK
IT'S NONE OF YOUR DAMN BUSINESS.
...
YOU'VE ADDED MORE EARRINGS.
FEH!
YUP, TWO MORE IN THE CARTILAGE.
YAY YAY
EARRINGS, HUH?
OOH! YOU INTERESTED? I'LL PIERCE YOURS.
THOSE LOVELY VIRGIN EARS OF YOURS, SOU.
YAY
Each ear has...
...seven!
Fourteen total!!
LOOK AT THOSE PRETTY EARS.
YOU'VE NEVER PUT HOLES IN THEM, HAVE YOU?
NOT IN MY EARS.
WHAAAT? WHAT'S THAT?! SOUNDS LIKE A DEEP, DARK SECRET!
THEN WHERE DO YOU HAVE HOLES, YOU KINKY BOY?
DON'T GET ALL EXCITED.
SO FOR EARRINGS, DO YOU USE A NEEDLE OR SOMETHING?

...
HEY!
OH MY GOD? OH MY GOD!
WHAT ARE YOU THINKING?! THAT KID?! NO WAY!
A KID?
HEY.
YOU'RE NOT THINKING...
YOU COULDN'T JUST DO IT QUICK WITH A PIERCING GUN?
NEEDLE ?!
DON'T USE SOMETHING THAT THICK!
Hmm.
YEAH.
EVEN A KID COULD WORK A PIERCING GUN.
I GUESS A NEEDLE WOULD BE DIFFICULT.
CAN YOU LISTEN FOR ONCE?
I do have it though.
KIO.
DO YOU HAVE YOUR PIERCING GUN WITH YOU?
FWAAA

...WERE SCARY, BUT NOW I THINK THEY'RE BEAUTIFUL.
I USED TO THINK...
...BUDDHIST ALTARS...
CHING
THE PURE WHITE CHRYSANTHEMUMS...
THE LIGHT OF THE CANDLE...
IT'S ALL SO BEAUTIFUL.
RIT-SUKA.
DINNER TIME.
COMING!

DO YOU LIKE IT, RITSUKA?
UH-HUH.
IT'S GOOD.

CLINK
CLINK

...
OOPS, DID I JUST STEP ON A LANDMINE?
I...
...don't know.
MNCH
MNCH

TWITCH
OH...

...HAVE EATEN THIS...?
I just ...
...don't know.

HOW WOULD "RITSUKA"...

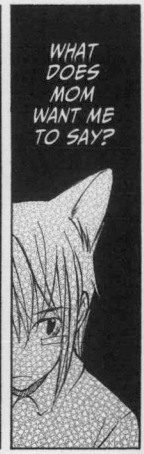
WHAT DOES MOM WANT ME TO SAY?

WHAT'S THE RIGHT ANSWER?

STOP IT, MOTHER.
THIS ISN'T RITSUKA ...
BUT SEIMEI, YOU'RE WRONG !!
THAT ATTITUDE OF YOURS ONLY PUTS MORE PRESSURE ON RITSUKA.
BUT ...
SEIMEI ...
I...
YOU'RE FINE JUST THE WAY YOU ARE, RITSUKA.
DON'T TRY TO FIND THE RIGHT ANSWER.
THERE'S NO SUCH THING.
DAD!!
IT'S ALL RIGHT, MISAKI.
DON'T YOU FEEL BAD FOR YOUR MOTHER?
KNOCK IT OFF.
SEIMEI, YOU TOO.
MISAKI ...
WHY WON'T YOU LISTEN TO ME?!
AND YOU, SEIMEI! WHEN DID YOU BECOME LIKE THIS ?!
CALM DOWN ...
MOTHER !!
DON'T CALL HIM RITSUKA !
STOP IT! STOP IT!
HE'S NOT RITSUKA.

YOU! YOU COULD NEVER UNDER-STAND...
IT'S ALL RIGHT.

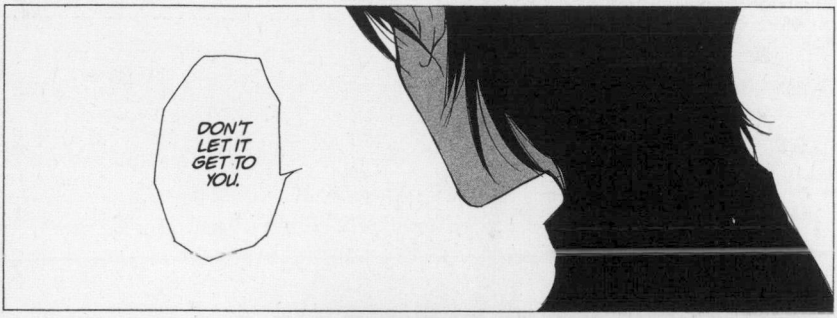
DON'T LET IT GET TO YOU.

YOU HAVEN'T DONE ANYTHING WRONG, RITSUKA.

BUT WHY IS THERE SUCH A BIG DIFFERENCE...
I DO EVERYTHING I CAN.
WE'RE SO DIFFERENT ON THE INSIDE.
W-WHAT?
UH, WELL...
I MEANT TO TELL YOU TOMORROW IS PARENTS' DAY AT SCHOOL.
!!
FLINCH
UH.
...AND ME, RIGHT NOW?
...BETWEEN THE "RITSUKA" OF TWO YEARS AGO...
I GUESS IT MAKES IT EVEN WORSE FOR HER.
NO WAY!
THAT'S IMPOSSIBLE. HE HAS WORK.
DAD, I THINK.
WHO'S SUPPOSED TO GO?
WHO...
WHAT?
...BUT FROM MOTHER'S POINT OF VIEW...
WE LOOK THE SAME ON THE OUTSIDE...
TWITCH
TWITCH

I'M SORRY.
I'M SORRY.
YEAH, I FIGURED.
YOU DON'T HAVE TO COME.
I have good grades anyway.
ZWEE
TAK
HERE'S SEIMEI'S COMPUTER.
INFORMATION ABOUT SEPTIMAL MOON...
.... SHOULD BE INSIDE.
OKAY.
THIS IS THE PROBLEM.

KREE
SIGH ...
I'VE BEEN CHECKING FOR BACKUP DISKS TOO.
Not here.
Not here.
AT LEAST...
...I THOUGHT IT WOULD BE.
"A PERFECTLY GOOD REASON."
"SO THAT YOU'RE NEVER LONELY, RITSUKA."
...
"CALL ME ANY TIME."
A WATCHED PHONE NEVER RINGS.
STARE
CHAK
FWAAA

DRIP
IF YOU WANT TO HEAR MY VOICE...
...YOU SHOULD JUST CALL ME.
BDMP
YOU HOPE THAT I'M COMING, DON'T YOU?
CHAK
WELL, TODAY ...
THEN WHY LEAVE IT UNLOCKED ?
FWAP
I DON'T.
WHY DO YOU ALWAYS COME IN THROUGH THE WINDOW ?!
THAT'S NOT AN ENTRANCE !

I HAVE A FAVOR TO ASK YOU, RITSUKA.
No umbrella?
I don't believe it.
YOU'LL CATCH A COLD!
Use an umbrella!
WHAT ...?
BUT FIRST...
...DRY YOUR-SELF OFF.
IT'S A BEAUTIFUL EAR, ISN'T IT?
AND NOW...
LOOK.

I WANT YOU TO PUNCH A HOLE IN IT.
What?
ERK
...
Punch a hole?
WHAT?!
THAT'S RIGHT.
PIERCE IT.
MAKE ME YOURS, RITSUKA.
HERE.
WUP
I FIGURE THAT USING A NEEDLE WOULD BE TOO MUCH, SO I BROUGHT THIS.
YOU WANT ME TO PIERCE YOU?! PUNCH A HOLE?! ME?!
WHAT?!
NO WAY!
I CAN'T DO THAT!!
JUST HOLD IT HERE.
YOU CAN.
NO!
I MEAN... YOUR EARS...
IT'S YOUR BODY! YOUR BODY!
Sterilized Piercing Devices
Stainless steel piercing
Titanium Long Type
Hypo-allergenic
WOO

TUG
I CAN'T DO THIS...
...IS JUST A FLESH WOUND.
PIERCING ...
Ick!
No!

IT'S A SYMBOL.
...IT WILL LEAVE AN INDELIBLE MARK.
IF YOU DO IT GENTLY ...

!
IF YOU DO IT FOR ME, THEN EVERY TIME I LOOK AT IT I'LL BE REMINDED OF YOU, RITSUKA.

!!
IT'S A WAY OF MAKING MEMORIES.

NGH...
YOU CAN DO IT, RITSUKA.
TUGH

I'M SCARED...!!
I DON'T WANT TO... I CAN'T.
WON'T IT HURT YOUR EARS?

I DOUBT IT.
THERE ARE A LOT OF THINGS...
...THAT HURT MUCH WORSE.

No!
Ngh!
Ears are so soft...
SWF
BE FIRM.
HEH
CHRK
THAT'S IT. RIGHT THERE.
IF YOU DON'T PUNCH THE HOLE QUICK AND CLEAN...
...IT'LL HURT A LOT MORE.
Hm?
HCOK
!
THEN GO AHEAD AND ENJOY THE PAIN!
OH.
GOT IT.

WHIP
NEXT!
THE LEFT EAR!
NGH...
STING
CHOK
NGH!
HUFF
SOUBI... DO YOU LIKE PAIN?
PEOPLE LIKE THAT ARE CALLED "MASOCHISTS."
SHAKE
SHAKE
DOES IT HURT?
SHAKE
SHAKE
NO.

NO.
I HATE PAIN.
HE LOOKS SO CALM...
YOU'RE ALWAYS LYING.
THANK YOU, RITSUKA.
THIS MAKES ME HAPPY.
SLUMP
THEN...
OBEY ME.
I WILL.
ASK ANY-THING.
SKWEEZ..
SEPTIMAL MOON ...
THERE'S ONLY ONE THING I WANT.
FIND THE PEOPLE WHO KILLED SEIMEI...!

FZZT
TAK TAK
ZZT ZZT
I CHECKED EVERY-WHERE IN THE COMPUTER AND THROUGH HIS OLD DISKS...
...BUT THERE'S NOTHING ELSE.
"I WILL BE KILLED BY SEPTIMAL MOON."
THERE'S ONLY THIS ONE MESSAGE ABOUT SEPTIMAL MOON.
OR SOMEONE ELSE?
CLICK
WHO ERASED IT?
SEIMEI ?
HIS EMAIL IS A RED FLAG, THOUGH.
EVERYTHING'S BEEN ERASED. THAT ISN'T NORMAL, IS IT?
MAIL
MAIL
0 ITEMS
537.7 MB FREE

SOUBI.
YOU...
YOU KNOW SOMETHING ABOUT SEPTIMAL MOON, DON'T YOU?
TELL ME!
SHAKE
I CAN'T.
SNAP
What ?!
WHY YOU...!!
DAMMIT !
YOU SAID TO ASK ANYTHING!

ON THAT PARTICULAR SUBJECT, I HAVE ORDERS FROM HIGHER UP.
I AM NOT ALLOWED TO ANSWER QUESTIONS PERTAINING TO SEPTIMAL MOON.
WHY NOT?
MRGH
I JUST CAN'T.
IF YOU ARE NOT PLEASED, RITSUKA...
...FEEL FREE...
...TO PUNISH ME.
GET OUT OF HERE!
SKRUT
I DON'T WANT TO SEE YOUR FACE!
...
CHAK
!!
W...
WAIT.
SHFF

RITSUKA ...
DON'T CALL ME.
I DON'T WANT TO SEE YOU.
I... I'M SICK OF THINKING ABOUT YOU ALL THE TIME, SOUBI.

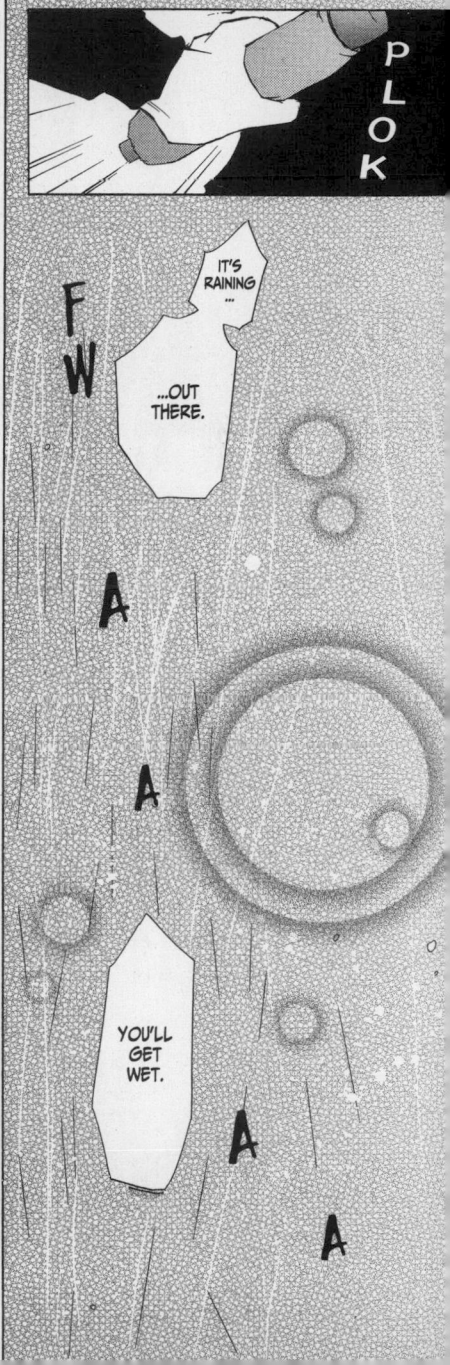
PLOK
IT'S RAINING ...
...OUT THERE.
FWAAA
YOU'LL GET WET.
AA

I WANT TO SEE YOU.
I DON'T WANT TO SEE YOU.
I LOVE YOU, RITSUKA.
OF COURSE I DO.
IT...
IT'S EXHAUSTING!
RITSUKA...
YOU THINK ABOUT ME ALL THE TIME?
HE'S DOING IT AGAIN, KILLING ME WITH SWEET WORDS!

MAKE IT AN ORDER.
COM-MAND ME.
PLEASE ...
RITSUKA.
TOMORROW'S PARENTS' DAY, RIGHT?
SHALL I GO FOR YOU?
FLICK
!!
HOW DID YOU KNOW...?
I TALKED TO YUIKO ON THE PHONE.
IF YOU WANT ME TO LISTEN TO YOU...
NO WAY, SOUBI...
I DON'T WANT YOU TO COME!
REALLY ?
OF COURSE NOT!!

GO...
GO HOME ALREADY!
DON'T COME TO PARENTS' DAY!!!
IF YOU UNDERSTAND, THEN GO HOME!

...
I UNDER-STAND.
FWAAA
I'LL GO HOME.

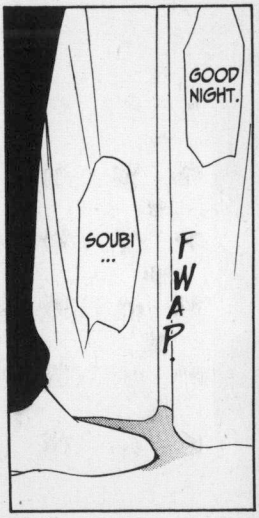
GOOD NIGHT.
SOUBI ...
FWAP.

CHAK
THANK YOU.
FOR THE UM-BRELLA.

DON'T GET WET.
DON'T CATCH A COLD.
THAT'S ...
...AN ORDER!
YES, SIR.
FWAAA

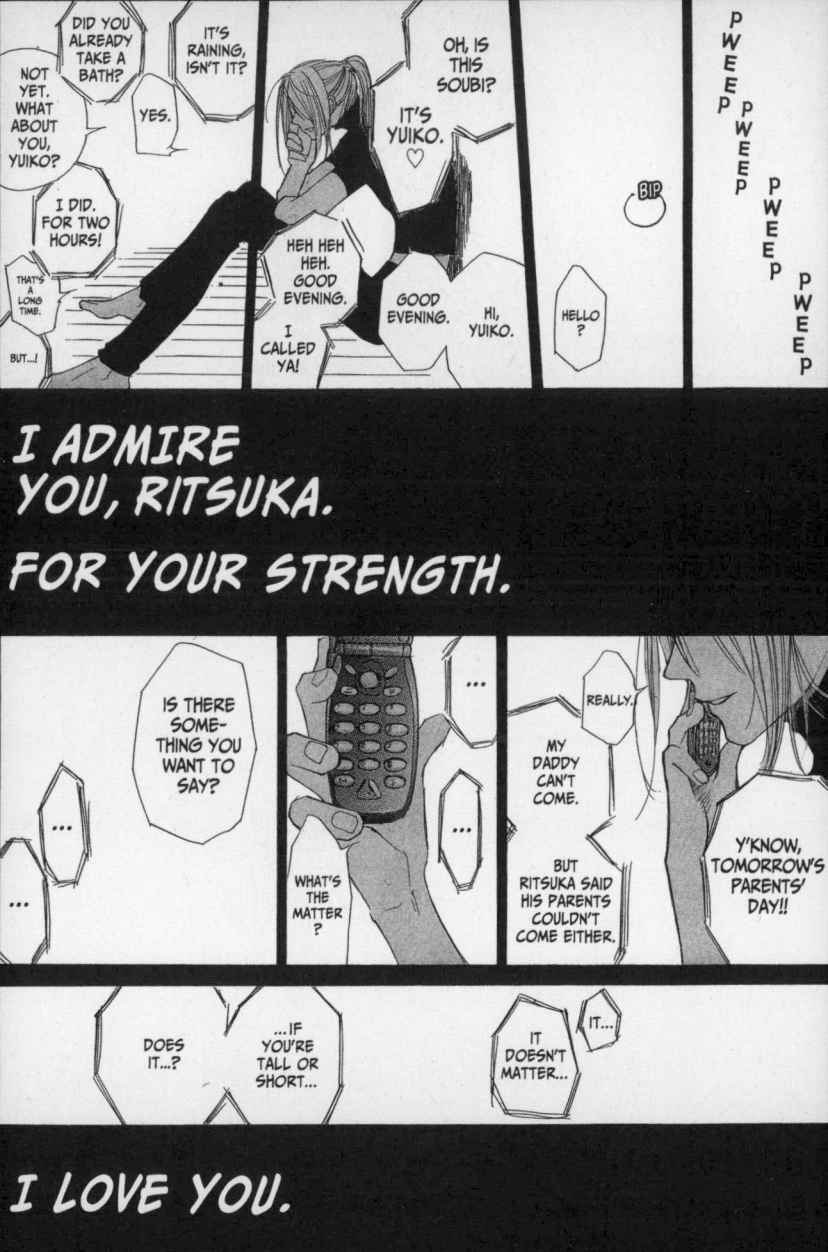
DID YOU ALREADY TAKE A BATH?
IT'S RAINING, ISN'T IT?
NOT YET. WHAT ABOUT YOU, YUIKO?
YES.
I DID. FOR TWO HOURS!
THAT'S A LONG TIME.
BUT...!
OH, IS THIS SOUBI?
IT'S YUIKO. ♡
HEH HEH HEH. GOOD EVENING.
I CALLED YA!
GOOD EVENING.
HI, YUIKO.
BIP
HELLO ?
PWEEP PWEEP PWEEP PWEEP
I ADMIRE YOU, RITSUKA.
FOR YOUR STRENGTH.
IS THERE SOME-THING YOU WANT TO SAY?
...
...
...
WHAT'S THE MATTER ?
...
REALLY.
MY DADDY CAN'T COME.
BUT RITSUKA SAID HIS PARENTS COULDN'T COME EITHER.
Y'KNOW, TOMORROW'S PARENTS' DAY!!
DOES IT...?
...IF YOU'RE TALL OR SHORT...
IT DOESN'T MATTER...
IT...
I LOVE YOU.

SEIMEI TOLD ME TO.

SOUBI.
IF I WERE EVER TO DIE, YOU WOULD THEN BELONG TO RITSUKA.
AFFIR-MATIVE.
SEIMEI TOLD ME TO... SO I WENT TO RITSUKA.
BUT I HAD NO IDEA... ...THAT HE WOULD BE LIKE THIS.

CHIRP
CHIRP
I HAD NO IDEA...
...THAT I WOULD GROW TO LOVE HIM SO MUCH.

Papers: Big Sky, Starry Sky; Shooting Star

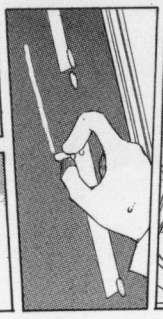

Thank you very much!
CLAP CLAP
OF COURSE, MY FATHER DIDN'T COME.
NEITHER DID YUIKO'S.
RITSUKA, LET'S GO HOME.
I'M SO HAPPY, TOMORROW'S A DAY OFF.
Whee!

DO YOU WANT TO HANG OUT TOMORROW?
HM? TO MAKE MEMORIES?
UH... WELL... SURE...
FLIK
HMPH HMPH HMPH!
Well, of course he didn't.
I told him not to!
SOUBI DIDN'T COME EITHER!!

CAN I...
...COME TOO?
It's Yayoi.

YOU WANT TO MAKE MEMORIES WITH ME?
Weird
What a weirdo.
?
?
MEMO-RIES ?
SOME-THING LIKE THAT... I GUESS.
AND I WANT TO GET TO KNOW YOU BETTER, AOYAGI.
HMPH
ME?
YOU TWO AREN'T DATING, RIGHT?
RIGHT.
Uh... uh-huh.
THEN I CAN'T GIVE UP ON YUIKO.
I DON'T MIND STARTING OUT AS FRIENDS.
I SEE.
I SEE!
Okay!
SO YOU WANT TO MAKE MEMORIES.
LET'S DO IT!
VRRRT
YUIKO WANTS TO GO TO KINUTA PARK.
OKAY. THEN ...
WHAT'S HIS DEAL?
PERK
What ?

AOYAGI, YOUR PHONE'S RINGING.
VRRRT
UH...
YEAH.

BDMP...

HE'S RITSUKA'S... UH... SERVANT?
I THINK ?
Servant ...?

I'LL BET IT'S SOUBI.
WHO ?
UH...
VRR...

SORRY !
DASH
I'LL CALL YOU ABOUT TOMORROW LATER!
HUH? HUH?
OKAAAY!

YES?
SOUB!!
HUFF
WHA...
WHAT ARE YOU DOING HERE?!
YOU DIDN'T TELL ME NOT TO COME PICK YOU UP.
CHK
AND YOU DIDN'T TELL ME TO NEVER COME SEE YOU AGAIN EITHER.
BY THE WAY...
...YOU ALSO NEVER TOLD ME NOT TO LOVE YOU, RITSUKA.
OR ARE YOU GOING TO FORBID THAT FROM NOW ON TOO?

FEH!
WHAT-EVER.
...
THEN...
OKAY...
BLUSH
SHALL WE GO?
I WAS THINKING WE COULD TAKE MORE PICTURES TODAY.
SOUNDS GOOD!
MY FRIEND SWIPED ALL THE PICTURES FROM BEFORE.
?
I'LL PRINT OUT ANOTHER SET.
THANK YOU, RITSUKA! I LOVE YOU.
LOVELESS 1 /END

HMM.

PANEL BORDER

INSERT PAGE NUMBERS HERE

THIS IS MY SPECIALIZED THUMBNAIL PAPER. IT'S REALLY CONVENIENT TO USE. B5 SIZE.

Do you want to die?

You mean you're serious about goofing off, or being a serious pain in the butt?

WHAAAT?

It's start-ing!

Oh no!

ULP!

THUMB-NAILS

I'll work hard, so please give us your support!!

Thank you for buying *Loveless* volume 1.

Layout

I love you, sleep.

ZZzzz...

KANJI CHARACTER QUIZ

USING CELL PHONE AS A PILLOW

Backstage epilogue, starring the manga artist and editor

Yun Kouga

Loveless begins!

CLAP

CLAP

CLAP

CLAP

Yes.

MANGA ARTIST

In Profile

About the blurb for *Loveless*.

So.

Like a sheep

SCRIPT

EDITOR S

First of all, I'm always serious.

Hey, now!

How about "This time Yun Kouga gets serious!"

You like it?

I am!

You always miss deadlines!! Liar!! You have no marketable skills other than drawing manga, so get cracking!!
You slow-poke!! Slacker!!
You stalker !!
Pervert !!
GRR GRR GRR GRR
PWEEP PWEEP PWEEP PWEEP
I'm really looking forward to your pages. ♥
Please, I'm asking ♥ nicely.
SEA OF BLOOD
Why do you lie?
Of course not.
You were sleeping, weren't you?
Hello, this is Kouga.
BDMP BDMP BDMP
Now you know the wonderful, collaborative atmosphere in which *Loveless* is created.
We hope you support us for a long time.
• www.ichijinsha.co.jp ← Home Page
• www.kokonoe.com ← my website
...
After lunch you said you needed to take a walk for a change of pace, and went to buy some books and drink tea and then after getting back you slept for two hours and after taking a shower and eating a snack you went to sleep again, didn't you?
I hope you read volume 2 as well! ♥
NOT THE WINGS OF AN ANGEL, BUT OF A FLY!!
It's no use. I've hidden the camera in a place where you'll never find it.
RSTL
SHUFF
SHUFF

I feel like I've changed a bit since starting work on *Loveless*. How so? You'll have to read on and see for yourself!

—*Yun Kouga, 2002*

loveless_yunkouga_2002_comic:zerosum_ichijinsha

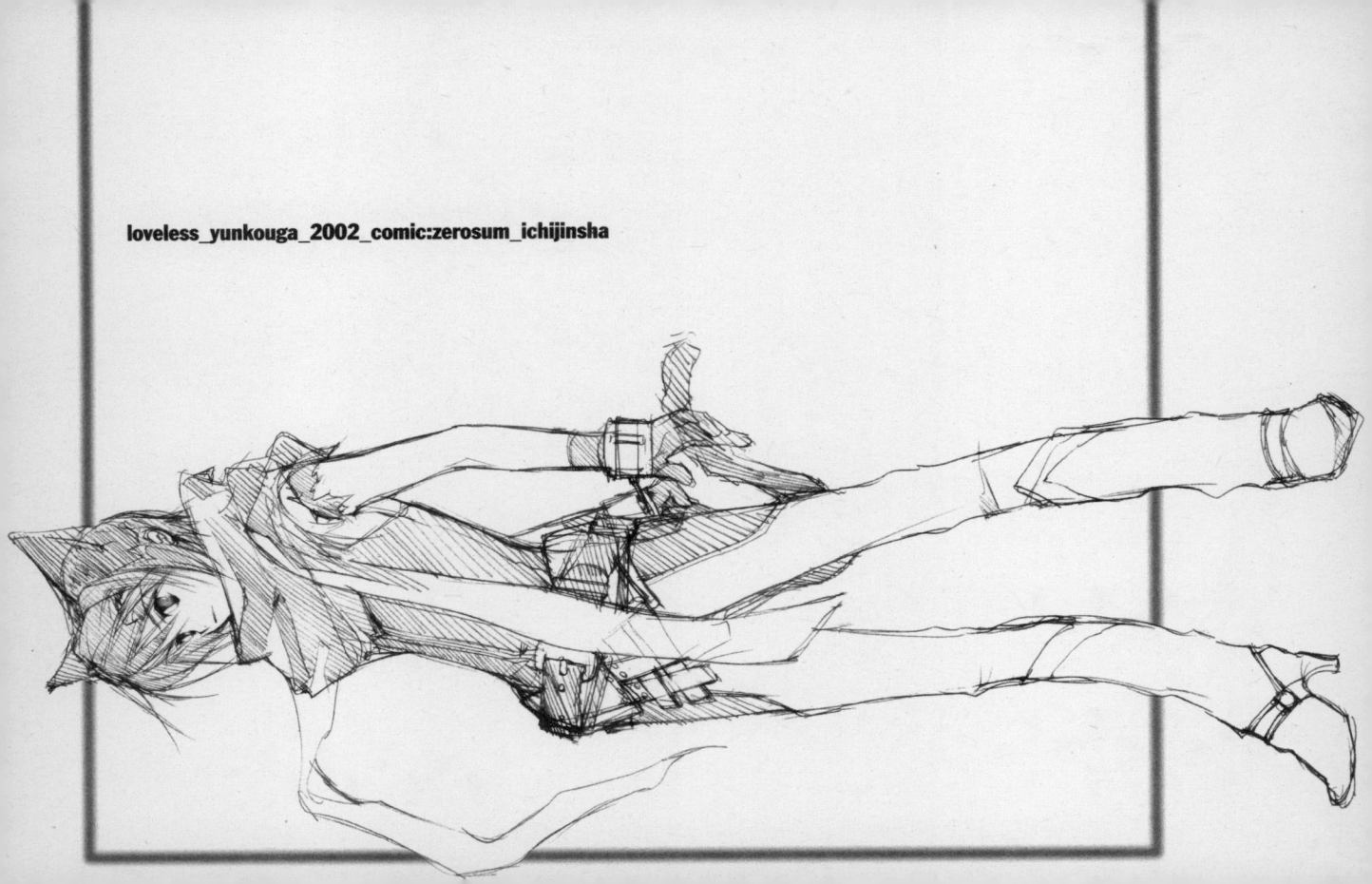

The following content ran as a SPECIAL LIMITED EDITION BOOKLET sold with *Loveless* volume 1.

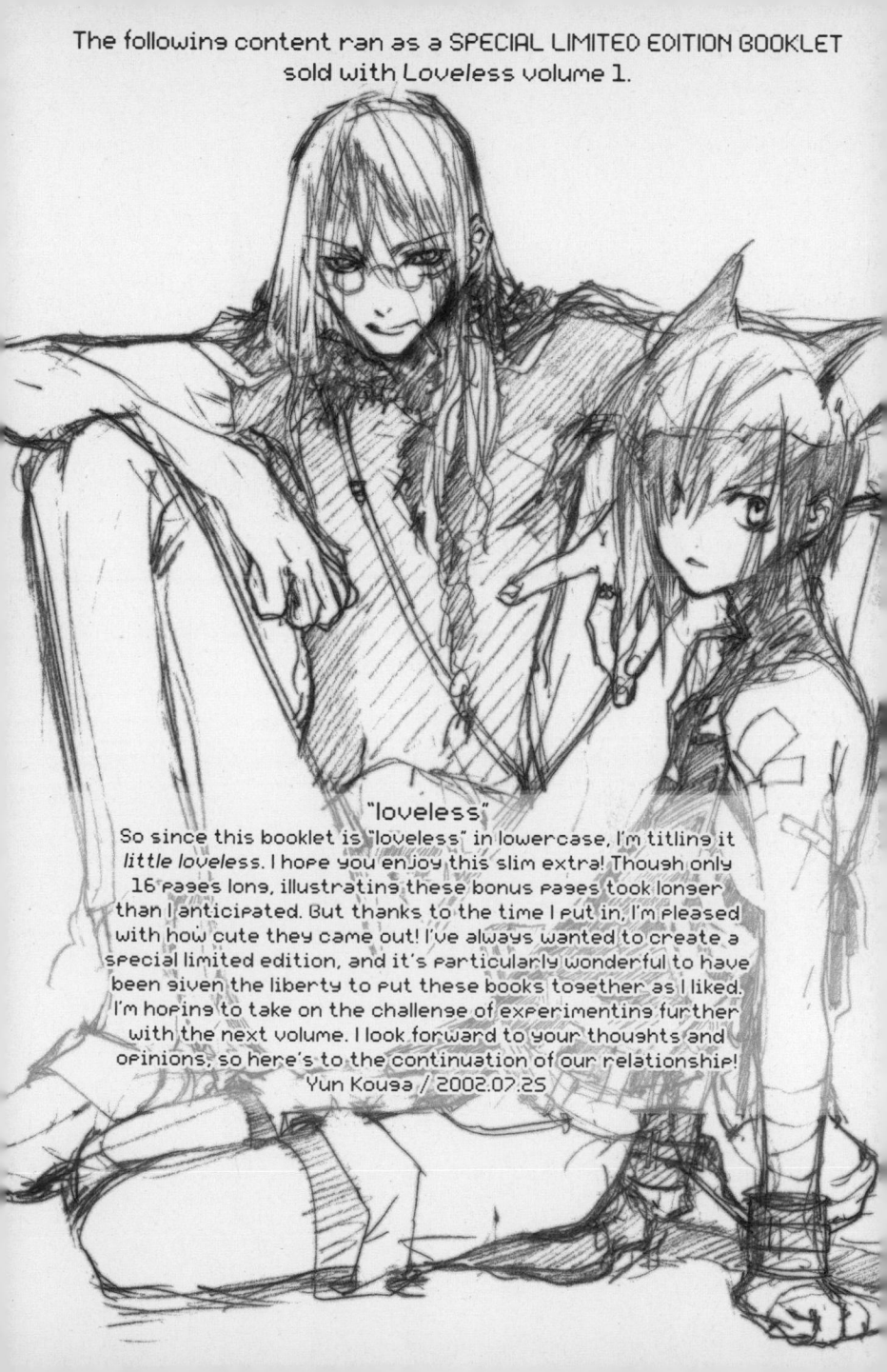

"loveless"

So since this booklet is "loveless" in lowercase, I'm titling it *little loveless*. I hope you enjoy this slim extra! Though only 16 pages long, illustrating these bonus pages took longer than I anticipated. But thanks to the time I put in, I'm pleased with how cute they came out! I've always wanted to create a special limited edition, and it's particularly wonderful to have been given the liberty to put these books together as I liked. I'm hoping to take on the challenge of experimenting further with the next volume. I look forward to your thoughts and opinions, so here's to the continuation of our relationship!

Yun Kouga / 2002.07.25

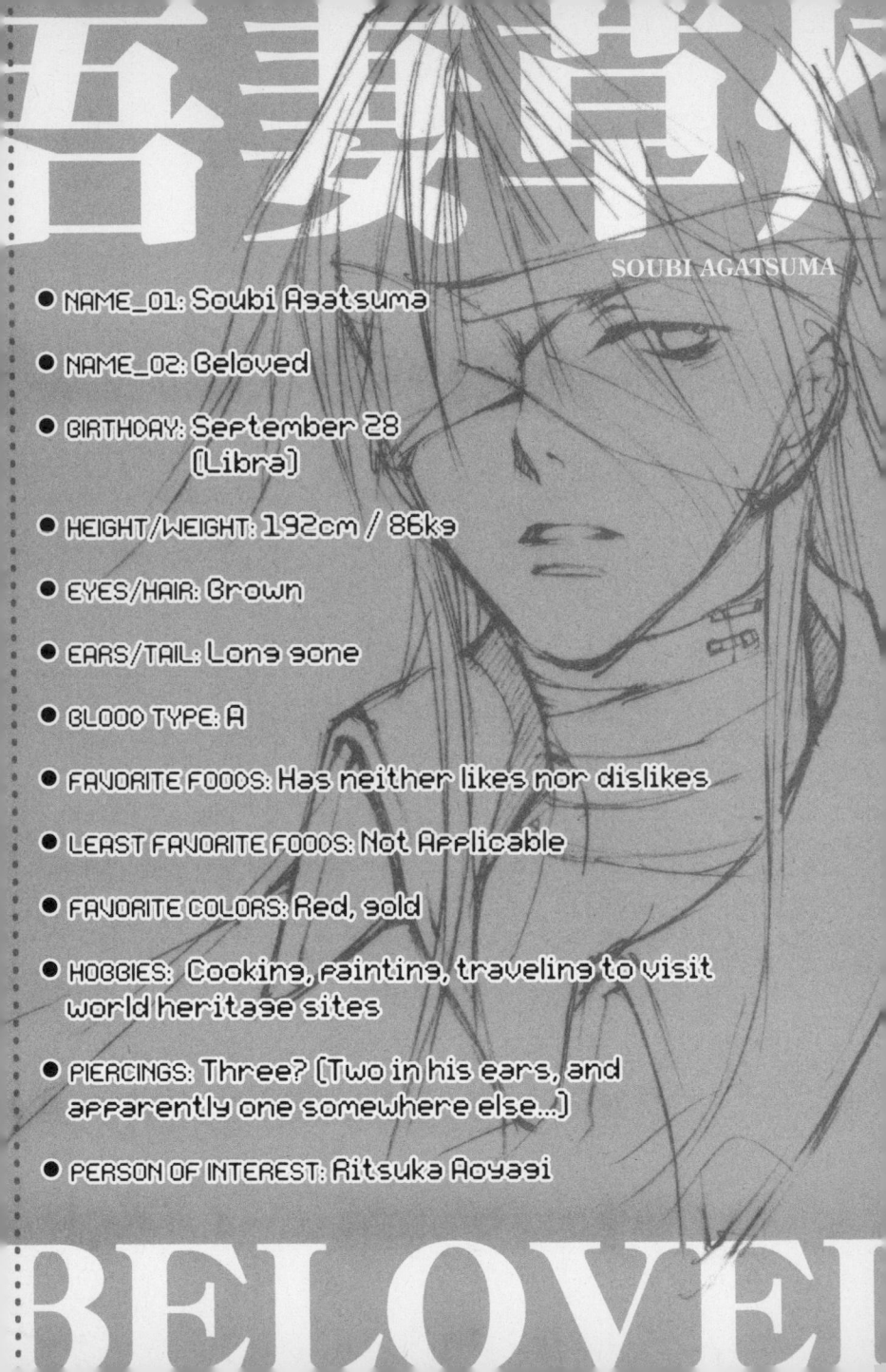
吾妻宗
SOUBI AGATSUMA
NAME_01: Soubi Agatsuma
NAME_02: Beloved
BIRTHDAY: September 28 (Libra)
HEIGHT/WEIGHT: 192cm / 86kg
EYES/HAIR: Brown
EARS/TAIL: Long gone
BLOOD TYPE: A
FAVORITE FOODS: Has neither likes nor dislikes
LEAST FAVORITE FOODS: Not Applicable
FAVORITE COLORS: Red, gold
HOBBIES: Cooking, painting, traveling to visit world heritage sites
PIERCINGS: Three? (Two in his ears, and apparently one somewhere else...)
PERSON OF INTEREST: Ritsuka Aoyagi
BELOVE

青柳立夏

RITSUKA AOYAGI

- NAME_01: Ritsuka Aoyagi
- NAME_02: Loveless
- BIRTHDAY: December 12 (Sagittarius)
- HEIGHT/WEIGHT: 147cm / 31kg
- EYES/HAIR: Black
- EARS/TAIL: Present
- BLOOD TYPE: B
- FAVORITE FOODS: Soft foods, anything from McDonald's, convenience store rice ball bentos
- LEAST FAVORITE FOODS: Too many to name, very picky eater
- FAVORITE COLORS: Shades of blue, white
- HOBBIES: Making memories
- PIERCINGS: None
- PERSON OF INTEREST: Soubi Asatsuma

LOVELESS

HANDWRITING BATTLE

SUGINO vs. KOUGA

Wa ha ha! Master Sugi mentioned that he dislikes writing by hand, so I blackmailed him into doing it.♡

Kouga: Hello!! Kouga here!! (I'm the manga artist!!) Today I'll be chatting with my editor.
≻Applause!≺

Sugino: Hhhhello! I'm Editor Sugino... I've never done something like this before, so I'm really nervous... Pleased to be here.

Ⓚ: Editing is a really tough job, isn't it? Especially when you get coerced into stuff like this. By the way, no corrections allowed.

Ⓢ: I mean, I'm still new to this sort of work. So, uh, how's it going? Volume 1 is on sale!

Ⓚ: (Why is your handwriting getting smaller?!) So you HATE Soubi, right, Master Sugi?

Ⓢ: That's not true. Even you were saying, "He's creepy..." ...So about the graphic novels...

Ⓚ: I gave the special limited edition books my best effort. There are things I wish I could have done, but I'll leave those for the next time!!

Don't give me a hard time!

Ⓢ: You really did put a lot of work into them! What shall we do for the next one? ...This is a misspelling, right?

Ⓚ: We'll do another one of these conversations.

Ⓢ: ARE YOU KIDDING ME?! Writing is hard :(

Ⓚ: Says the person who remembers to bring Hanazono dumplings every day but forgot a pen for this conversation...

Ⓢ: I didn't think we were going to go through with it...Was the monaka tasty?

Ⓚ: Weak! (I'm not talking about the monaka... That was delicious.) When I say I'm going to do something, I do it. Hey, what did you think the first time you saw the storyboards for this manga?

Ⓢ: They were interesting. I thought, "Wow! This is Yun Kouga!" Although during our first meeting I did feel like I was being sexually harassed. lol

Ⓚ: (...? What about the storyboards...?) That's what you think of me?

Ⓢ: (Storyboards first, huh?) I think that you are, forgetting logic for the moment, all about coolness & cuteness & eroticism.

Ⓚ: What's with you, Master Sugi?! You're not going to tell me to die or yell that you're going to kill me today??

Ⓢ: That's all I've been saying... I wonder if you're going to stay true to form for the rest of your life in that you "can't hit deadlines"!

Ⓚ: What? But I always hit my deadlines. (There, I said it! Now, how many people will actually believe it? *FIDGET FIDGET*) ᵘᵤ

Ⓢ: Uh, sure...(deadpan) Well, you do try your best each month. (← Does she have something on me?)

Ⓚ: In any case, I'm glad that you like Loveless, Master Sugi. You do, right?

Ⓢ: I'm a big fan! Please stay interested in it. (← **his true feelings?**)

Ⓚ: Is it okay to ramp up the eroticism? (trying to secure a promise)

Ⓢ: As long as it's fun! Of course anything goes... But there are limits. Anything we have to put a censor mosaic over would be too much. (← **Oh, c'mon.**)

Ⓚ: There's nothing erotic about a mosaic. (Whuh?)? I want to get the second volume out within the year.

Ⓢ: I see, I see! Let's do our best! For as long as we live!! ...Which would be now...

Ⓚ: Master Sugi has a blog online at Zero-Sum's website, so everyone please check it out! See ya!!

Ⓢ: What the hell?! :D Well, like it or not, this is the artist of Loveless, so please favor us with your ongoing support.

Say what?!

If I die, let it be by your words.
LOVELESS
Congratulations on the release of volume 1!
The combination of "loser adult and levelheaded child" is a big-time hook for me. I totally look forward to it every month. I'm so glad to be working for *Zero-Sum.* :D
Ms. Kouga, please allow me to join you for drinks again. I'd love to talk about work with you! Thank you for asking me to contribute this guest art. It really feels like a milestone for me. But I'm sorry I couldn't make Ritsuka sufficiently cute... (sweating) Next time I hope you can draw lovely portraits of my children...!! :D
KAZUYA MINEKURA 2002

A tidbit...
Yun Kouga, embarrassed as never before, and my rude self.
Um, so ears... y'know, ears ...?
I was thinking about the lead in this next manga, and I thought I'd try out some ears...
After I drew some c-cat ears I couldn't stop going down that path, and it was like, what the hell, but...
One day, in Yokohama
Wait, but why cat ears?
Are they going to let me draw a peculiar manga like that...?
Huh?
Ms. Kouga, when have you ever drawn a manga that wasn't peculiar?
100% True Story
YURI NARUSHIMA
CONGRATS ON VOLUME 1!!
CLAP
CLAP

Yayyyy!!! O-did you see that?! Did you see it?!
Our guests for the commemorative first volume were Yuri Narushima and Kazuya Minekura. I'm so happy! Please continue to bless us with your kindness!
Ms. Minekura! Your portrayal of a tough, scrappy Ritsuka and the lovably pathetic loser-adult Soubi (hee hee) is just what I'd expect from you!! I promise to repay this kindness! I'm certain that it will go over big with the readers too.
I hope to see you again in volume 2.
We are published monthly in Zero-Sum, so please support the magazine as well. You must be thinking I don't have anything else to say. But hmm, I don't. A big thank-you to all you readers and to the people who helped make this!

YURI NARUSHIMA http://www.naruri.com/top.html
KAZUYA MINEKURA nitroblog.exblog.jp
YUN KOUGA http://www.kokonoe.com
ZERO-SUM / ICHIJINSHA http://www.ichijinsha.co.jp/

loveless
BLEH! NO WAY, NO WAY!!
I'M NEVER EATING FERMENTED SOY-BEANS!
HISS
HISS
ME NEITHER! NUH-UH! NOT GONNA EAT 'EM!!

SO WHAT DO YOU DO ABOUT SCHOOL LUNCHES?
I NEVER EAT 'EM.
I NEVER EAT 'EM.
THEN WHAT DO YOU LIKE TO EAT?
SOFT STUFF.
Chewing's a pain.
PUDDING AND ICE CREAM. AND STRAWBERRIES TOO.
DUMBFOUNDED
I'M DUMBFOUNDED.
LISTEN TO YOU TWO.
IT'S ALWAYS "CAN'T EAT THIS, CAN'T EAT THAT."
ANYTHING FROM MCDONALD'S.
AND THE RICE BALL BENTO FROM 7-11.
ME TOO!
OKAY, STOP.
I'LL WHIP UP SOMETHING WITH WHATEVER'S AVAILABLE.

AFTER SCHOOL...
SZZZL
...SOUBI OCCASIONALLY COOKS FOR US AT YUIKO'S HOUSE.
SZZZL
...
SINCE WE'RE REALLY PICKY EATERS, HE GETS KINDA MAD AT US.
Y'KNOW, SOUBI ...
YOU ALWAYS SAY THAT YOU'LL DO WHATEVER I WANT.
SO WHY TRY TO FEED ME STUFF THAT I DON'T LIKE?

NATTO FRIED RICE

Ingredients!!
(for 3 servings)

Natto (pre-packed fermented soybeans): 3 packages

Ground beef/pork mix: 100–200g

Green onion: about 5 cm

Dried bonito, salt, soy sauce, oil to taste

Rice: 3 cups

1 Prepare the natto. (mix in the green onion and soup base)

MIX IT UP!

2 Fry the ground beef/pork mix in an oiled, heated frying pan.

SEASON WITH SALT AND PEPPER

3 Add the rice (leftover rice is fine!) and natto and stir fry!

SEASON WITH THE DRIED BONITO

FINISHED!

It doesn't look like much, but it's tasty!!

※ CAUTION!

Natto is already seasoned, so use additional salt sparingly.

※ If you mix too vigorously after adding the natto, it will become sticky. Stir briskly.

BARF!
DON'T MIX UP STUFF I LIKE WITH STUFF I HATE!
ULP!
TURN
BUT YOU LIKE TUNA, RIGHT?
I'LL ADD THIS, SO EAT UP.
BUT WHY?
I HATE VEGE-TABLES.
I HATE IT!!
WHAT ABOUT ASPAR-AGUS?
GRRR!
IT'S JUST FATE !!
I DON'T GET IT...
GREEN SALAD
3. Dress everything with the spicy tuna.
If you like, you can squeeze in a lemon. If you don't have the spicy kind of tuna, add a bit of soy sauce and Chinese chili oil.
Do Steps 1 and 2 at the same time.
1. Cut up the vegetables.
Use a slicer for the cucumbers.
2. Boil:
Asparagus: 1-2 minutes is good.
•Green soybeans:
CUT HERE
You can cut them up using scissors, like they do in fine restaurants (ha ha). Boil to semi-hardness.
Boil in a small amount of water for 5 to 6 minutes!! You can also add wakame seaweed and onions.
•Broad beans:
If you make an incision in the middle with a knife, they won't shrink when you boil them.
Ingredients!!
Anything green is OK.
• Cucumbers
• Broad beans
• Asparagus
• Green soybeans
• Peas
• Green beans
• Can of tuna fish (spicy!)
BECAUSE OF THE DRIED SARDINES IN IT...
WHY'S THAT?
I DO...
DO YOU LIKE MISO SOUP?
NO WAY!
I CAN'T EAT NATTO FRIED RICE.
YOU'LL BE FINE.
MISO SOUP WITH BEAN SPROUTS AND DEEP-FRIED BEAN CURD
If making soup stock with dried sardines, it's fine to remove the head and stomach.
The one point to consider:
Prepare a regular deep-fried bean curd miso soup, and top it off with bean sprouts stir-fried in sesame oil!!
Delicious!
But don't simmer the bean sprouts in the miso soup.
It's just a simple miso soup with bean sprouts and deep-fried bean curd.

CHOMP
!
NGH...
NO
IT'S GOT DRIED BONITO IN IT!
JUST HUMOR ME, AND TRY ONE BITE.
IT'S GOOD!
!!
MUNSCH MUNSCH
...
...
...
CHOMP
NO.
I CAN FEED MY-SELF.
MY LOSS.
BLUSH
SMILE
Isn't it?
HERE.
TRY ANOTHER BITE.

TOFU JELLY

Ingredients:
- gelatin
- milk
- silken tofu
- sugar

1. Blend the tofu in a blender!!
2. Melt the gelatin in warm milk.
3. Mix in the blended tofu, season with sugar, and chill!!

It's even better if you have a cute mold to put it in! A drizzle of honey goes well on top.

It works with soy milk too!

I THINK SOUBI LIKES PRETTY THINGS.
THAT'S VERY PRETTY.
AND HE DOESN'T HAVE EARS... SOMETIMES I REMEMBER HE'S "ONE OF THEM"...
SWIP
SWIP
WE HAVE TO RESTORE THE KITCHEN BACK TO THE WAY IT WAS.
IF HER MOM FINDS OUT, WE'LL GET IN TROUBLE.
SOME-TIMES HE FEELS LIKE "ONE OF US"...
RUSTLE
RUSTLE
IT'S STRANGE THAT SOUBI CAN PREPARE FOOD SO EASILY AT SOMEONE ELSE'S HOUSE.

I'M IN THE ARTS AND CRAFTS CLUB.
WE'RE MAKING CELL PHONE CHARMS.
YOUR CELL PHONE LOOKS BARE, RITSUKA.
SO...
ME ?!
Leave me...
...out of this.
FLICK
FLICK
YOU'RE PRETTY GOOD!
I'M JUST PUTTING BEADS ON A STRING.
BUT THE COLORS ARE NICE.
YOU HAVE GOOD COLOR SENSE, YUIKO.
HUUUH?
REALLY ?
DON'T JUST PRAISE EVERYTHING!!
That's too nice.

FEH!
AWW...
YOU'RE A TOUGH CUSTOMER, RITSUKA.
BLUNT
YOU DON'T NEED TO SAY EVERYTHING!
BUT THAT'S WHAT I THINK.
SHOULDN'T YOU SAY WHAT YOU FEEL?
DRIP
DRIP
DRIP
DRIP
DRIP
C'MON, RITSUKA. RITSUKA!
WHAT DO YOU WANT?!
RITSUKA, RITSUKA!
...SHUT UP.
FLK
FLK
FLK
SMILE

WHAT THE HELL IS THIS?!
I THOUGHT YOU WERE AN ARTIST!
I AM AN ARTIST.
LIAR!

GRR!
HERE.
RITSUKA

THIS DRAWING IS TOTALLY WEIRD!
GAG!
WHAT DO YOU MEAN? IT LOOKS JUST LIKE YOU.
NO!!
IT DOES NOT!!
HUH?! IT DOES LOOK LIKE YOU! IT'S SO CUTE!! ♡

THEN I SHOULD HEAD HOME TOO.

THAT'S MOM'S "COMING HOME" CALL.
IT MEANS SHE'S ON HER WAY HOME.
BRING...
RINGALING...
OH.

YUIKO, LOOK...
BRING
AH.
RIT

FWAAAA
...IS TO LEAVE NO TRACE OF OUR PRES-ENCE.
SORRY, THE FIRST RULE OF YUIKO'S HOUSE...
FWAA
WANNA TAKE AN UMBRELLA?
IT'S RAINING SUPER HARD.
SPSH
SPSH
...
MAYBE YOU'RE FINE, BUT...
WE'LL BE FINE LIKE THIS.

!
TRMBL
IT'S PRETTY ...
... CHILLY.
IT'S WARM.
...
SOUB!'S BOD.%.
ARE YOU STILL COLD?
...YOU CALL SOME-THING LIKE THIS?
YOU LOOK COLD-BLOODED.
SO WHY ARE YOU SO HOT?
I WONDER WHAT...
DON'T CLING TO ME.
YOU'RE ALL HOT.

YOU SAID YOU WERE COLD, RIGHT?
SKWEEZ
Everyone always says it's nice...
...that I run so hot.
I DON'T LIKE IT.
YOU'RE HOT.
AHH, I KNOW.
IT'S LIKE THAT TIME I HELD A HAMSTER IN THE PALM OF MY HAND.
LIKE A HAMSTER.
SO WARM AND SOFT.

SO NICE THAT I COULD CRY.
IT'S KIND OF A NICE FEELING...
FWAA

little loveless 1 / END

LOVELESS

YUN:KOUGA_LOVELESS_2003

Chapter 1 223
Chapter 2 273
Chapter 3 311
Chapter 4 337
Chapter 5 365
loveless -in the summer- part 1 385
loveless -in the summer- part 2 393
BONUS: little loveless 2 413

PUNISHMENT
DOMINATION CRUELTY
HEY!
SOU, YOU'VE GOT PIERCINGS!
YOU WENT AND DID IT! WHEN'D THAT HAPPEN?
YOU LOOK GOOD.
THEY'RE KINDA GAY.
'CAUSE I'M A MORNING PERSON.
YOU REALLY LIKE BUTTERFLIES DON'T YOU, SOU? YOU ALWAYS HAVE THEM AROUND.
WHY ARE YOU PERKY SO EARLY IN THE MORNING, KIO?
BUTTER-FLIES?

TOY'S MASTER / VOLUME OF THE ABSOLUTE TOY MASTER

CHAPTER 1

"Toy"
—*noun*. An instrument of play; an object of amusement; a plaything; a person or thing to be played with for the purpose of enjoyment.

TOY

"Coerce"
—*verb*. To compel obedience through the threat of force; to dominate or control.

COERCE

I HATE THEM.

ABSOLUTE

"Absolute" (definition • uses)
—*noun*. Having no equal; having no comparison; a state of perfection; a state of supremacy; to rely on nothing; to face no limitation; unconditional. *Philosophical:* An absolute being
—*adverb:* Absolutely; unconditionally; certainly; by any means.

UH.
I SEE.
...
BUT...
...YOU'RE PAINTING BUTTERFLIES RIGHT NOW, AREN'T YOU?
WHAT'S THERE TO HATE? THEY'RE BEAUTIFUL.
I HATE THAT THEY'RE BEAUTIFUL.

NO ONE CARES ABOUT CATCHING HAIRY CATERPILLARS.
AND I HATE THE FACT THAT THEY'RE SO EASILY TRAPPED.
IS IT SO EASY?
IT'S AWFUL HOW THEY WIND UP AS SPECIMENS WITH PINS STUCK THROUGH THEIR ABDOMENS.
Whoa, touchy subject.
BUT THAT'S NOT THE BUTTERFLY'S FAULT...
I DON'T GET YOU, SOU. YOU'RE NOT MAKING SENSE.
DID SOMETHING HAPPEN?
SHUP
AH!
SOME-THING DID HAPPEN!
BDMP
TELL ME!
BDMP

RITSUKA.
SNAP! JUST LIKE THAT.
WHOA, HOLD ON A SEC.
HEY.
JUST WHO EXACTLY PIERCED YOUR EARS FOR YOU?
YOU MONSTER!
I FEEL BAD FOR THE KID.
BARF!
WHUH?!
YOU MADE A LITTLE VIRGIN KID DO IT!
GYAAAAH!
PICH

MAN, OH MAN...
NO MORE PERVERTS FOR ME TODAY.
I'M GOING TO MY PART-TIME JOB.
DID I TELL YOU ABOUT MY NEW GIG?
OHH HOO!
SHUF...
HAVE FUN.
I HAVE TO DO CRAZY THINGS IN THE NUDE IN FRONT OF A WHOLE CROWD OF PEOPLE.
RUB RUB
I'M SURE YOU'RE SPECTACULAR AT IT.
WHUMP
HANG ON... WHAT'S THAT SUPPOSED TO MEAN?
SOU, YOU REALLY DON'T GIVE A DAMN ABOUT ME, DO YOU?!
GRR
GRR
YOU SURE ACT LIKE YOU COULDN'T CARE LESS!
I WOULDN'T MIND SEEING YOU NAKED, KIO.
GRR

YOU'RE AN ART MODEL, RIGHT?
I'D LOVE TO DRAW YOU.
I'M GOOD.
GET TO YOUR JOB.
WHEE
WHEE WHEE
I'D TAKE OFF MY CLOTHES FOR YOU ANYTIME!
DAR-LING!
BIP BIP BIP
BIP BIP
BIP
BIP BIP

MMR
BIP BIP
BIP
BIP BIP
GH

IT'S MORNING ...
YAWN
I'M SO TIRED...

SHUF

TOK.
MORNING, SEIMEI.
YOU'RE RELIEVED THAT SEIMEI'S DEAD, AREN'T YOU?
MISAKI ...
WHY WOULD YOU SAY THAT?
I'M NOT DUMB!
YOU'RE PATHETIC.
WHAT A MISERABLE MAN.
SEIMEI WAS STRONGER THAN YOU'LL EVER BE.

STOP TRYING TO STIR THINGS UP.
SEIMEI WAS SO MUCH MORE OF A MAN THAN YOU ARE.
SEIMEI WAS SUPPOSED TO PROTECT ME.
MOM CALLED SEIMEI STRONG.
JUST LIKE MOM.
BUT THE SEIMEI I KNEW WAS KIND.
BUT NOW HE'S DEAD. IT'S ALL OVER!!
ME AND... RITSUKA ...
BAM
BAM
BAM
...TAKE ME AWAY FROM THIS PLACE!!
SEIMEI WAS GOING TO...

AT THE FUNERAL, THE PRIEST SAID DEATH WASN'T THE END.
BUT...
...IT'S OVER?
MY MEMORY OF HIM IS SO VIVID.
...
HE'LL HEAR ME.
IF I LIGHT INCENSE EVERY DAY...
...AND PRAY...
SEIMEI IS STILL "HERE."
WHEN YOU DIE, THAT'S THE END!!
CRASH
OVER!!
IT'S OVER!!
...
ARE YOU STUPID?

GLUNK
MOTHER!
LOOK!
HE CAN'T DO ANYTHING ANYMORE!
NOTHING STAYS BEHIND!
VSH
WHAP
!
BSH
SMASH
BSH
M...!
YANK
LOOK!
WHAT CAN SEIMEI DO FOR YOU NOW?!
HE WON'T SAVE YOU!
NOBODY IS COMING TO SAVE YOU!

YOU'RE NOT GOING TO STOP ME?
YOU HAVE TO STOP ME!!
WHAT'S YOUR PROBLEM ?
YOU'RE RUNNING AWAY?!
KLAT
I WON'T MOVE.
I CAN'T PROVOKE HER... SHE'LL ONLY HIT ME AGAIN...
HE CAN'T DO ANYTHING!
!!
HE'S GONE!
SEIMEI'S DEAD!
...TO STOP ME!!
SWSH
THAT'S WHY...
THERE'S NOBODY...

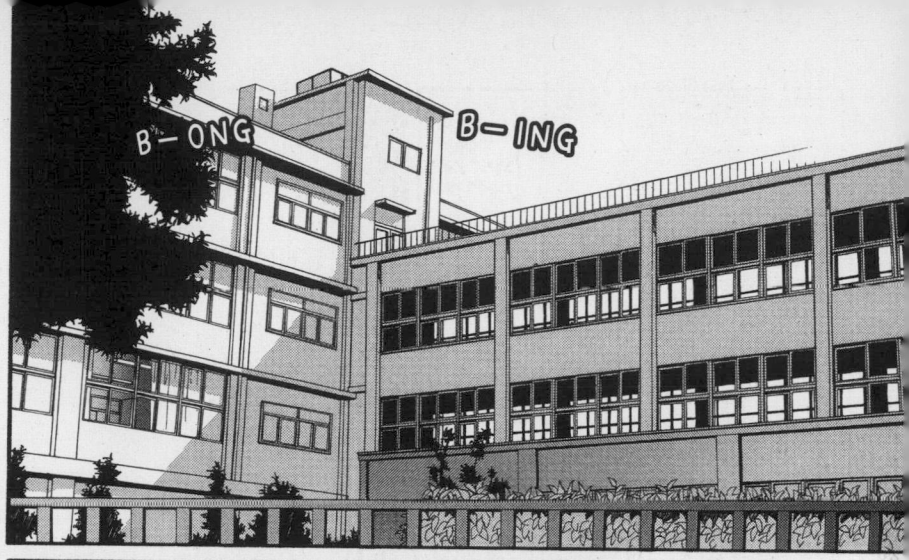
B—ONG
B—ING

NOW MOVE ALONG TO THE MUSIC ROOM DURING THE TEN-MINUTE BREAK.
SKRUT
SKRUT
BOW!
ATTENTION!
THANKS, EVERY-ONE!
THAT'S ALL FOR NOW.

I WONDER WHY? IS HE JUST TARDY...?
MURMUR
MS. SHINO-NOME! RITSUKA DIDN'T COME!
MURMUR

SOMETHING MUST HAVE HAPPENED.
RITSUKA'S NEVER TARDY.
BUT...
HE'LL COME TODAY...
I KNOW HE WILL.
HE PROMISED.
HEY, HEY! ♡
RITSUKA, GET THIS!
KREE
ALL THREE OF US, AS A FAMILY.
KREE
I'M LISTENING.
SO WE WENT TO PICK STRAWBERRIES THIS WEEKEND.
ME, MY MOM AND DAD—THE THREE OF US!!

THE LAST TIME I WAS IN FOURTH GRADE.
BUT STRAWBERRY SEASON WAS OVER, SO EVEN THOUGH WE WENT, THERE WERE HARDLY ANY LEFT!
KREE
KREW
MY PARENTS FINALLY GOT THE SAME DAY OFF!
HUH.
KREE
I WANTED TO EAT A HUNDRED, BUT THERE WAS NO WAY.
IT'S ALL GOOD!
WE COULDN'T EAT THAT MANY STRAWBERRIES, ANYWAY.
THAT'S TOO BAD.
KREE
WE JUST LAUGHED.
DADDY HAD BEEN SO PUMPED UP, HE WAS SO DISAPPOINTED.
I DON'T REALLY LIKE STRAWBERRIES.
She's hard-core.
FOR REAL?!
I LOVE STRAWBERRIES.
YOU THINK? I GOT NICE AND FULL!
SIGH
BUT EVEN I COULDN'T EAT A HUNDRED.
You'd get a stomach-ache!
Yikes.
THAT'S KIND OF SCARY, ACTUALLY.

SO... IT'D BE OKAY IF THEY WERE SWEET?
YEAH, SWEET IS OKAY.
...
...
...
GLANCE
?
What?
NUH-UH!
HOW COULD ANYBODY NOT LIKE STRAW-BERRIES?
THEY'RE SOUR.
BUT THEY'RE SO TINY AND DELICIOUS!
NO WAY! WHY NOT?!
Is it really that shocking?
Geez.
YOU JUST KEEP STIRRING AND STIR-RING.
IT'S KINDA...
I MEAN, THE COLOR ISN'T NICE LIKE THE KIND THEY SELL, BUT IT TASTES GOOD!
HEH HEH HEH!
IT'S 100% HOME-MADE!
YOU KNOW... WELL...
AFTER WE GOT HOME, I MADE JAM WITH MY MOM.
ME?
I WANTED TO GIVE YOU SOME, RITSUKA.

WHEE!
THEN I'LL BRING IT TO SCHOOL TOMORROW.
Secretly!
COOL.
...
SURE.
UH-HUH.
DON'T WORRY. IT'S REALLY SWEET.
YOU WANT SOME ...?
HE SAID HE WANTED IT...
SLUMP
...
TO RITSUKA

EWW! WHAT THE HELL IS THIS?!
NO!
STOP IT!!
GIVE IT BACK!
TMP TMP TMP TMP
BLEH!
DUMP IT! IN THE TRASH!
GIVE IT BACK! GIVE IT BACK!
NO!
IT LOOKS LIKE POOP. IS IT EVEN EDIBLE?
EWWW!
STOP IT!
HEY!
YOU CAN'T BRING THIS TO SCHOOL!
GIVE IT BACK!
IT SAYS, "TO RITSUKA" !!
EWWW!
WHAT IS THIS?
JAM, I GUESS?
NO...!!
PEEK
WANT A TASTE FIRST ?
NO WAY! GROSS!
HA HA HA!
BET YOU'D GET FOOD POISONING FROM THIS.

BRINGING STUFF LIKE THIS TO SCHOOL...
...IS AGAINST THE RULES.
GLOOP
GLOOP
GLOOP
!!
TUNK
NGH...
THERE YOU GO!! ALL GONE!!
ZWAAAAA

NGH...
PLIP
PLIP
AH...
AH...
NNGH...
WAAAAH!
OH SHUT UP.
WHAT'RE YOU CRYING FOR? IT'S YOUR FAULT.
IDIOT!
SHE MAKES ME SICK.
LET'S GO.
SNIFF...
SNF...
I...
I MADE IT FOR RITSUKA...
I WENT... TO PICK STRAW-BERRIES...
M...
MOMMY...
BWEHH!
HEY, DON'T CRY.
"WHAT? YOU'RE GIVING IT TO A BOY? GOOD FOR YOU, YUIKO!"
"HEH HEH HEH... THINK HE'LL LIKE IT?"
"OF COURSE HE WILL."

LICK
YOU'RE RIGHT.
IT'S GOOD.
TINK
YOU SHOULD HAVE KNOWN BETTER, YUIKO.
BRINGING SOMETHING LIKE THIS WAS AN INVITATION FOR THEM TO MAKE YOU MISERABLE.
R...
SNIFF
PLIP
PLIP
PLIP
SNIFF
SNIFF
WAAAH
R...
R...

BAM
大空
大空
ERK!
THIS HERE.
WHO DID THIS?
TO ATSUKA

...IT'S HER FAULT FOR BRING-ING IT!
BUT...
MURMUR
MURMUR
MURMUR
WHAT?
WHAT'S HE TALKING ABOUT?
RAR
AND YUIKO BROKE THE RULES!
RAR
IT'S AGAINST THE RULES!
IT'S A RULE.
HIC
YEAH, THAT'S RIGHT!
HIC
ARE YOU SAYING YOU'VE NEVER BROKEN THE RULES?
HMM.
SO IT WAS YOU.
YIKES
YIKES
YIKES
YUIKO DID SOME-THING WRONG!
THAT'S GOT NOTHING TO DO WITH IT...
IT'S YUIKO'S FAULT!
!!
MURMUR
HUH?
WHAT IS THAT?
GAR-BAGE?
WHAT'S GOING ON?
THAT WAS REALLY CRUEL.
IT MAKES ME DOUBT YOUR HUMANITY.

WHO GETS HURT BY YUIKO BRINGING THIS TO SCHOOL?
YUIKO DID NOTHING WRONG. SHE DIDN'T HURT ANYBODY.
TO RITSUKA
BUT YOU STILL WENT AND HURT HER.
PEOPLE WHO HURT OTHERS ARE A LOT WORSE...
...THAN PEOPLE WHO BREAK RULES.
I THINK YOU SHOULD ALL DIE!

ERK!
I KNOW HOW YOU FEEL.
BUT BREAKING THE RULES ISN'T RIGHT, EITHER.
AND YOU SHOULDN'T SAY THINGS LIKE THAT TO YOUR FRIENDS.
RITSUKA.
OOPS.
BIN-G
BON-G
HAWATARI, DON'T CRY...
BWUT MIZ ZINO-NOBE ...
SNIFF
SNURF
SNUFF
SNF
SNF
HIC
GUIDANCE ROOM

I'M SOOO SORRY!
I OUGHT TO HAVE GONE BY YUIKO'S HOUSE TO PICK IT UP.
SLUURP
RITSUKA.
IT'S AGAINST THE RULES TO STOP ANYWHERE ON THE WAY HOME TOO!
...
MS. SHINO-NOME.
IT'S WAY WORSE TO HURT SOMEONE'S FEELINGS THAN TO HURT THEIR BODY.
THAT'S WHAT I THINK.
RITSUKA ...
THANKS FOR THE SNACK!
CHAK
HEY ...
RITSUKA, HOLD ON!
LATER, MS. SHINO-NOME.
SMILE
Moving along!

SNIFF
SNIFF
PACHAK
AH!
CAN'T I GET ANYTHING RIGHT?
GEEZ...
SIGH...
SNIFF
MS. SHINO-NOME?
SNIFF
HONK
YES.
UM.
CAN I TELL YOU SOME-THING?
I...
I REALLY LIKE RITSUKA.
MS. SHINO-NOME!

I THOUGHT HE WAS COOL AND ALL WHEN HE TRANSFERRED HERE.
I WANTED TO BE HIS FRIEND.
RITSUKA'S REALLY NICE TO ME.
BUT NOW, AFTER TODAY, I LIKE HIM EVEN MORE.
I WOULD DO ANYTHING FOR RITSUKA, BUT I DON'T KNOW WHERE TO START.
RITSUKA PROTECTED ME.
I'D DO ANYTHING FOR RITSUKA.
I'D EVEN DIE FOR HIM.
HAWATARI ...!
SHE DOESN'T KNOW YET...
...THAT THIS IS LOVE.

SHE MAY STILL BE TOO YOUNG TO COMPREHEND IT.
YEAH.
I UNDER-STAND.
BUT NO TALKING ABOUT DYING, OKAY?
UNH...
SNIFF
SNIFF
SNIFF
'KAY.
TO SAY YOU'RE WILLING TO DIE FOR SOMEONE...
THAT'S LOVELY.

MS. SHINONOME. I HEAR THERE WAS SOME COMMOTION IN YOUR CLASS TODAY.
WAS IT RITSUKA AOYAGI?
AH HA HA.
OH NO, IT WASN'T RITSUKA'S FAULT...
I think.
BUT...
...WHAT SORT OF CHILD IS RITSUKA?
HIS EYES ARE COLD.
HIS SMILE IS FORCED.
AND YET...
...HE'S VERY SENSITIVE TO OTHER PEOPLE'S PAIN.
UH...
IS THERE SOMETHING I SHOULD KNOW ABOUT RITSUKA IN HERE?
WELL, THAT FILE CONTAINS TRANSFER LETTERS AND REPORT CARDS...
...FROM HIS PREVIOUS SCHOOL.
AND HE'S BEEN BADLY HURT HIMSELF.

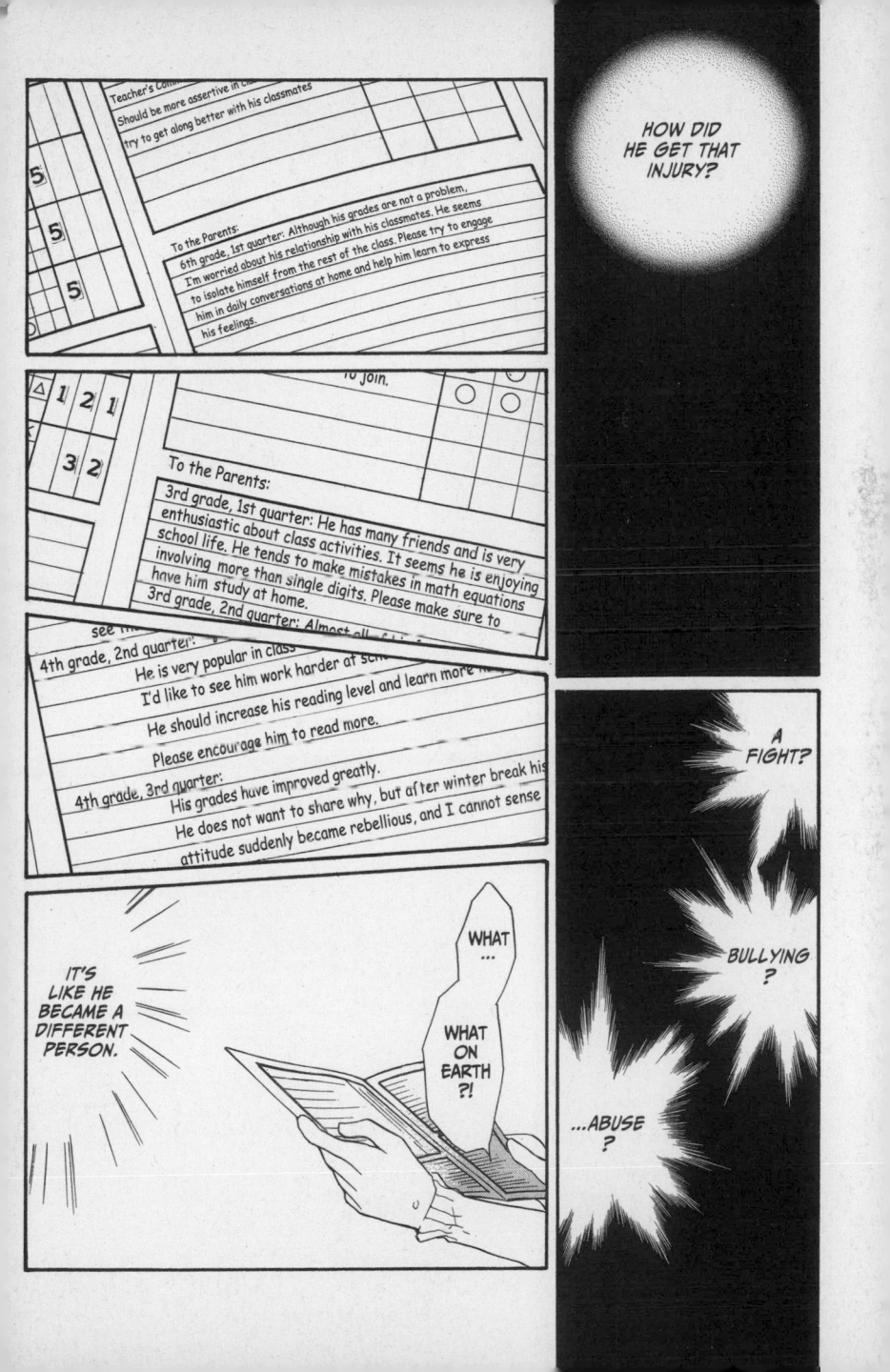
Should be more assertive in
try to get along better with his classmates
To the Parents:
6th grade, 1st quarter: Although his grades are not a problem, I'm worried about his relationship with his classmates. He seems to isolate himself from the rest of the class. Please try to engage him in daily conversations at home and help him learn to express his feelings.
To the Parents:
3rd grade, 1st quarter: He has many friends and is very enthusiastic about class activities. It seems he is enjoying school life. He tends to make mistakes in math equations involving more than single digits. Please make sure to have him study at home.
4th grade, 2nd quarter:
He is very popular in class
I'd like to see him work harder at
He should increase his reading level and learn more
Please encourage him to read more.
4th grade, 3rd quarter:
His grades have improved greatly.
He does not want to share why, but after winter break his attitude suddenly became rebellious, and I cannot sense
IT'S LIKE HE BECAME A DIFFERENT PERSON.
WHAT ...
WHAT ON EARTH ?!
HOW DID HE GET THAT INJURY?
A FIGHT?
BULLYING ?
...ABUSE ?

WHAT HAPPENED...?

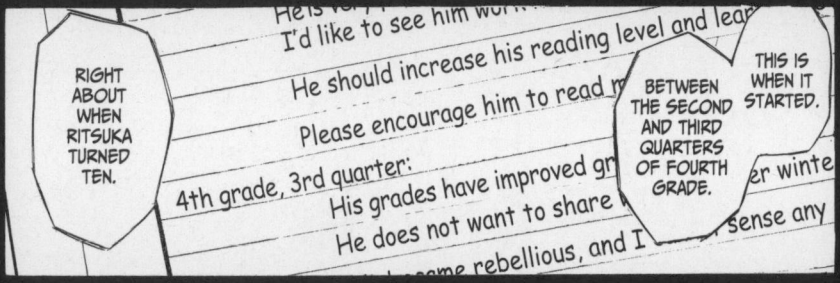

WHAT HAPPENED TWO YEARS AGO?

CAN PEOPLE CHANGE SO DRASTICALLY? AND IN SUCH A SHORT PERIOD OF TIME?

CAN SOMEONE BECOME A COMPLETELY DIFFERENT PERSON?

DON'T YELL LIKE THAT IN FRONT OF SOME-ONE'S HOUSE.
MY MOM WILL HEAR.
THEN COME TALK WITH US.
No way
...to enough.
HERE.
...
GLARE—
HEY! I DIDN'T PUT ANYTHING FUNNY IN IT!
YOU JUST SAW ME BUY IT!!
WHY WOULD YOU BUY ME ANY-THING?
As if.
EXCUSE ME?!
PLAP
THAT'S SO NOT CUTE!
ERK!
!

I'M FINE.
ARE THOSE CUTS INFECTED? THEY HURT, RIGHT?
LEAVE ME ALONE.
WHAP
YOU'VE GOT A FEVER.
FIGURES ...
AI?!

WE WERE TAKEN OFF THE JOB, SO WE AREN'T GOING TO FIGHT YOU ANYMORE.
HA.
YOU WANNA FIGHT?
DON'T WORRY ABOUT ME. ANYWAY ...
WHAT DO YOU WANT?

WE JUST DECIDED TO STOP BY AND SAY HELLO.
YOU REALLY DON'T KNOW ANYTHING, DO YOU?
OUTSIDE OF THE JOB, WE DON'T HAVE ANYTHING AGAINST YOU.

HUH?

NOT LIKE WE WANT TO SEE YOU ANYWAY.
SCHOOL ...?
WE'RE BEING SENT BACK TO SCHOOL.
AND I DON'T KNOW WHEN WE'LL GET TO LEAVE NEXT.
WE PROBABLY WON'T EVER SEE YOU AGAIN.
HE'S REALLY BAD NEWS.
LOOK... DON'T LET HIM FOOL YOU.
NOD
SOUBI ?!
SOUBI WENT THERE TOO.
A SCHOOL FOR FIGHTERS.

RSSH
...
ANY-WAY.
I'M SURE WE'LL BE REPLACED.
WHAT DID YOU DO TO SEIMEI ?!
YOU GUYS ARE JUST AS BAD.
BUT...
I KNOW THAT MUCH.
THE SCHOOL WILL SEND SOMEONE ELSE.
AND THAT TEAM WILL TAKE YOU DOWN!
AS IF I'D LET THAT HAPPEN!
I'M NOT GOING ANYWHERE!

BECAUSE IF THIS "RITSUKA" DISAPPEARS TOO, WHAT WOULD MOM DO...?
SWEAT
AWW, NOW WHAT?
A HOUSE CALL? IT'S KINDA SUDDEN.
HM?
I'M AT...
...RITSUKA'S HOUSE!!
BDMP
BDMP
BDMP
WHAT SHOULD I DO?
I JUST CAME HERE ON IMPULSE.
AOYAGI

OH MY! CIGARETTE BUTTS?
HMPH!
NO PUBLIC DECENCY!
Not cool!
OH!!
HE'S...
...MR. AGATSUMA!

MR. AGA-TSUMA ...
OH, CRUD!
BLUUUUSH
YES ...?
EEE!
AND YOU ARE?
WELL ...
I KNOW HIM...
AAUGH!
BLUSH
BLUSH
...BUT HE DOESN'T KNOW ME!
UH.
UM...
I... I...
I'M RITSUKA'S TEACHER ...
BLUSH
RITSUKA'S TEACHER ...?
AND YOU KNOW ME?
I SOUND SO SUSPICIOUS!
I'M A TEACHER AT YANO JONAN ELEMENTARY SCHOOL. MY NAME IS SHINONOME ...
WHAT SHOULD I DO?!

UH...
YES.
I SAW YOU AT THE SCHOOL GATE YESTERDAY, AND WHEN I ASKED...
...RITSUKA TOLD ME YOUR NAME.
RITSUKA TALKED ABOUT ME...
SMILE
SKFF
AND SO?
DO YOU HAVE BUSINESS WITH RITSUKA?
ER...
IS THIS A HOUSE CALL ?
WELL, UH...
I HAD SOME-THING ON MY MIND... BUT NO BIG...
WHA...
UH...
WHAT'S HIS DEAL?
IS HE REALLY A FRIEND OF RITSUKA'S BROTHER ?
I... UH...

HEY, MS. SHINO-NOME!
HOW OLD ARE YOU?
BDMP
HUH?
ME...? MY AGE?
BDMP
BLUSH
ME?
I'M 23.
23!
YOU'RE PRETTY OLD.
I DON'T REALLY GO FOR OLDER WOMEN.
KRAK
W...
BLUSH
WHA...
SOUBI!!

WHAT ARE YOU SAYING, MR. AGATSUMA ?!
BLUSH
THAT'S NEVER GOING TO HAPPEN!!

HEY!
WHY'D YOU SAY THAT?!
I COULD HEAR YOU!!

REALLY ?

RIT SUKA !

RIT-SUKA !

WHA...!! EXCUSE ME?!
IT'D BE ANNOYING IF SHE GOT A CRUSH ON ME, SO I HAD TO NIP IT IN THE BUD.

THEN DON'T CRY.
PLIP
PLIP
!!

ER...
MS. SHINO-NOME, ARE YOU OKAY?

...
PLIP

MS. SHINO-NOME, I'M VERY SORRY.
SMILE
Agh!

SOUBI !!
APOLOGIZE TO HER!
YES, SIR!

THIS IS...
WOBBL
...HUMILI-ATING!
DASH
MS. SHINO-NOME!
...
AUK...
THERE SHE GOES ...
WH... WHAT THE HELL WAS THAT?!
WHY DID YOU MAKE HER CRY?!
KARR
WHY...? I JUST TOLD YOU.
IT WOULD BE INCONVENIENT IF A PERSON LIKE THAT FELL IN LOVE WITH ME.
SOUBI !!
WHAT A MEAN THING TO SAY!
WHY ARE YOU LIKE THAT?
ARE YOU ANGRY ?

THEN...
PUNISH ME.
DO AS YOU SEE FIT, RITSUKA.
GO AHEAD.
ANY WAY YOU LIKE.
GRP
I...
...WILL NEVER...
...RAISE MY HAND AGAINST ANYONE!

I WILL NEVER USE VIOLENCE.

TOO BAD.
THIS IS MORE DISCIPLINE THAN VIOLENCE, THOUGH.

BY THE WAY... WHY WAS SHE AT MY HOUSE?
WHO KNOWS ...?
WHY ARE YOU HERE, SOUBI?
Just for a quick stalk.

I SAID NO, AND I MEAN IT!
NO!!
OKAY, OKAY.
GRR

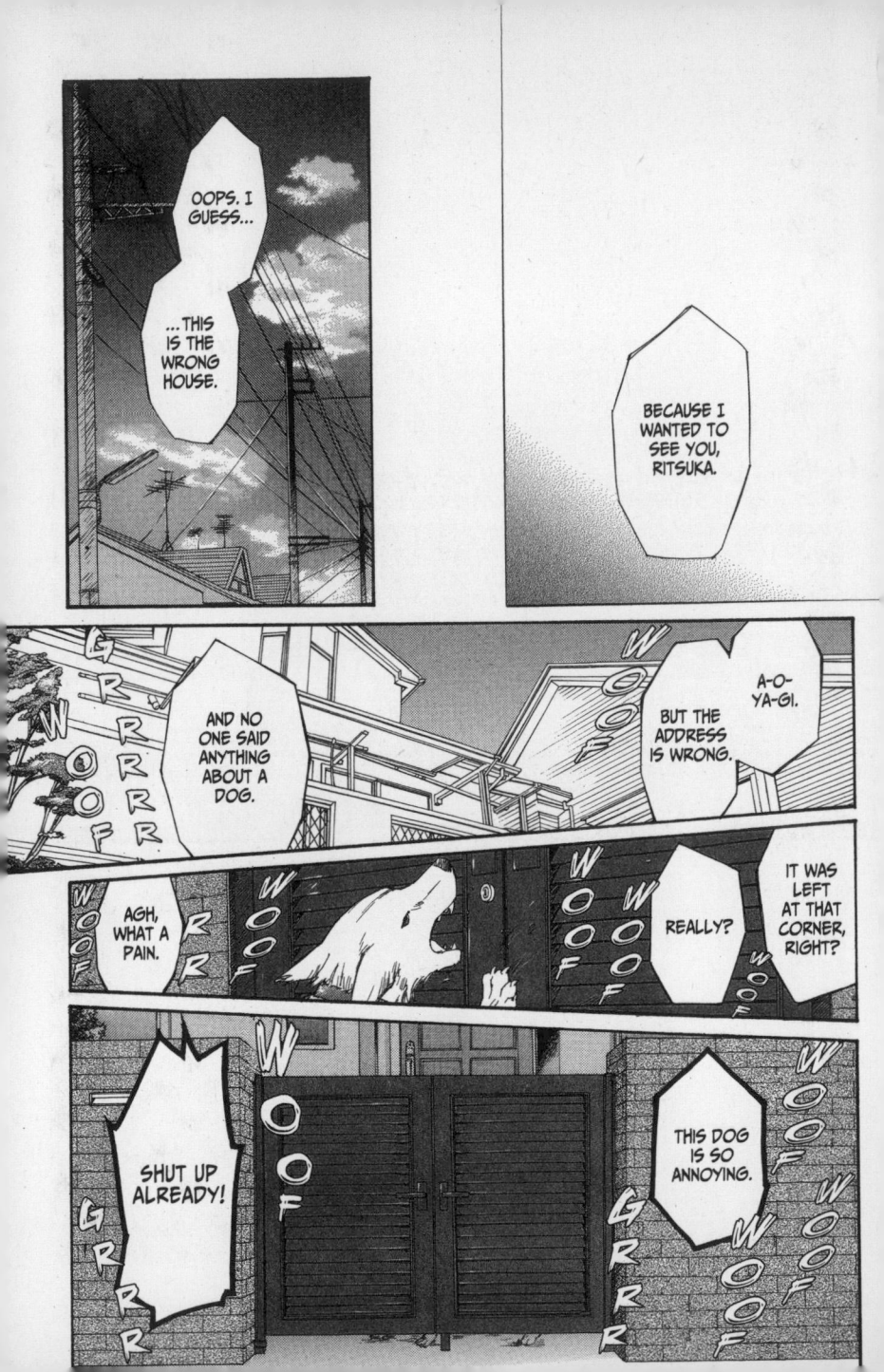
OOPS. I GUESS...
...THIS IS THE WRONG HOUSE.
BECAUSE I WANTED TO SEE YOU, RITSUKA.
A-O-YA-GI.
BUT THE ADDRESS IS WRONG.
AND NO ONE SAID ANYTHING ABOUT A DOG.
GRRRRR
WOOF
WOOF
IT WAS LEFT AT THAT CORNER, RIGHT?
REALLY?
AGH, WHAT A PAIN.
WOOF
WOOF
WOOF
WOOF
WOOF
WOOF
WOOF
WOOF
WOOF
WOOF
WOOF
WOOF
THIS DOG IS SO ANNOYING.
SHUT UP ALREADY!
GRRR
GRRR

KRAK!
PEEL!

SLSH
OOPS.
IT WAS ANNOY-ING.

THIS IS SUCH A HASSLE.
SERIOUSLY, MAN.
WHERE ARE YOU, RITSUKA AOYAGI?
I MEAN, DO WE JUST HAVE NO SENSE OF DIRECTION?

TOY'S MASTER / VOLUME OF THE ABSOLUTE TOY MASTER

CHAPTER 2

LET'S SEE.
WHAT'LL IT BE?
SUMMER MANDARIN JELLY?
OR YUBARI MELON CREAM SODA?
UGH.

MIDORI...
...YOU REALLY HAVE STRANGE TASTE IN SODA.
WHY DO YOU SAY THAT?
FINE, GET WHATEVER. THE BUS IS COMING.
OKAY, OKAY.

VROOM
FUTAGOTAMA
BUMMER...
I WON'T BE ABLE TO DRINK THIS ONCE WE'RE BACK AT SCHOOL.
...
WHO CARES...?
HEY!

AH.
TWITCH

HM?
TWITCH
WHAT IS IT, KIN?

WEEEEN
SOME-ONE'S CLOSE.
THERE'S A FIGHTER OTHER THAN SOUBI NEARBY.
IT'S NOT SOUBI?
NO, IT'S NOT...
THE BATTLE RADIUS IS TOO SMALL FOR IT TO BE SOUBI.
WHO IS IT?
THIS SMELLS FISHY...
THEY'RE HERE ALREADY. THAT WAS QUICK.
VROOOM
IT WAS QUICK.
BUT TOO BAD.

WE CAN'T DO ANYTHING NOW.
THEY'RE JUST GOING TO HAVE TO DEAL WITH IT ON THEIR OWN.
THAT KID...
...AND SOUBI.
THEY'RE GONE...
YEAH ...
GLUNK
VROOM
FUTAGOTAMA
SWISH
OH WELL.
IF THEY DON'T INTEND TO ATTACK, THEN I GUESS IT DOESN'T MATTER.

HE TOLD ME SOMETHING REALLY MEAN...
SINCE I HAD THE CHANCE, I ASKED HIM IF SOUBI HAD ANY WEAKNESSES.
YOU AND SOUBI, KINKA?
YOU'RE GOING TO FIGHT? THAT'S...
BUT I ASKED THE PRINCIPAL WHAT HE WAS LIKE...
...BECAUSE I HEARD HE WAS A GRADUATE.
MM-HMM.
AND SO?
KIN...
IS THIS SOUBI STRONG?
THAT'S WHAT I HEAR.
I NEVER FOUGHT HIM, SO I DON'T KNOW FOR SURE.

SOUBI'S WEAKNESS?

SOUBI HAS NO WEAK-NESSES.
HE IS PERFECT.
HE APPARENTLY THOUGHT IT WAS ONLY NATURAL...
...THAT SOUBI WOULD WIN.
GRRR GRRR
WHAT ?!

THE REASON SOUBI FIGHTS AT SUCH A HIGH LEVEL...
...IS BECAUSE HE CAN PICK HIS ATTACKS.
HE CAN CHOOSE TO APPLY PHYSICAL VIOLENCE ...
...OR DESTROY THE PSYCHE.

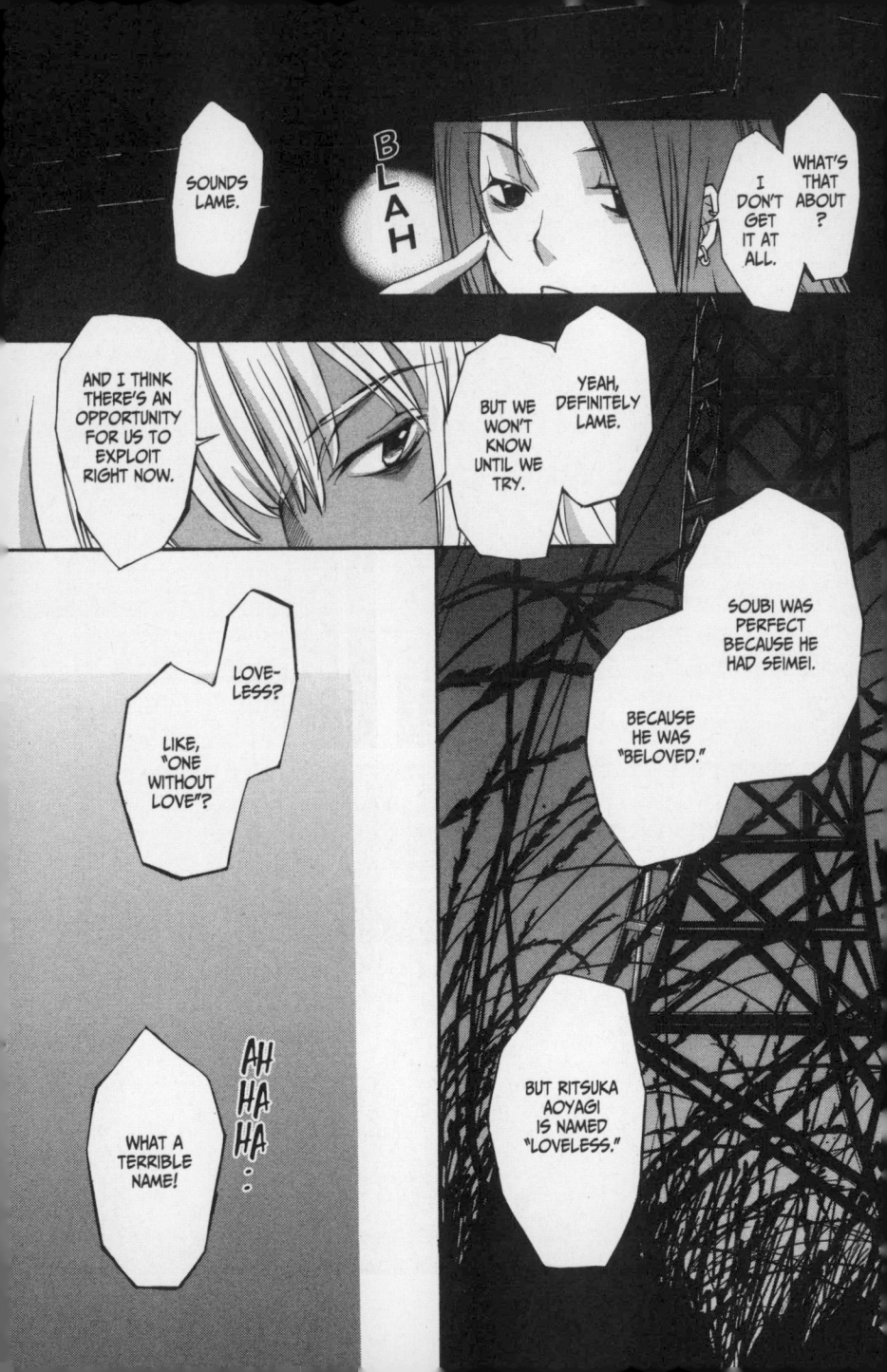
WHAT'S THAT ABOUT?
I DON'T GET IT AT ALL.
BLAH
SOUNDS LAME.
YEAH, DEFINITELY LAME.
BUT WE WON'T KNOW UNTIL WE TRY.
AND I THINK THERE'S AN OPPORTUNITY FOR US TO EXPLOIT RIGHT NOW.
SOUBI WAS PERFECT BECAUSE HE HAD SEIMEI.
BECAUSE HE WAS "BELOVED."
BUT RITSUKA AOYAGI IS NAMED "LOVELESS."
LOVE-LESS?
LIKE, "ONE WITHOUT LOVE"?
AH HA HA...
WHAT A TERRIBLE NAME!

THE SUN'S GOING DOWN.
WHY NOT?
I...!!
SOUBI, I DON'T THINK...
...
GO HOME.
BLUSH!!
I DON'T NEED YOU.
FLIK
...
YOU LIVE IN A NICE AREA.

YOU CAN'T FOOL ME WITH NICE WORDS.
YOU KNOW THINGS YOU WON'T TELL ME ABOUT.
WHY'S THAT ?
YOU'RE THE ONLY ONE FOR ME, RITSUKA.
...BUT I CAN'T!!
I WANT TO TRUST YOU...
...THAT I CAN TRUST YOU.

...
...
DO YOU WANT TO KNOW... RIGHT NOW?
YES, I WANT TO KNOW RIGHT NOW!!
SOUBI...
YOU ALWAYS ASK ME THESE PRYING QUESTIONS...
...BUT NEVER TELL ME ANYTHING ABOUT YOURSELF.
THAT'S NOT TRUE AT ALL.
Hands off!!
Hey!
I BELONG TO YOU, RITSUKA.
ALL OF ME.
SHEE...
SO I'LL...
...SHOW YOU EVERYTHING. WHAT DO YOU WANT TO SEE?

JOLT
GOT IT.
SHAAA
I'LL GRANT YOUR WISH RIGHT NOW, RITSUKA.
WHAT ...
TUG
BUT NOT HERE.
COME THIS WAY.
THERE'S AN ENEMY.
THEY'RE CLOSE BY. WHAT DO YOU WANT TO DO?
AN ENEMY ...
IS IT SEPTIMAL MOON...?
BAMP

KIN?!
TWITCH
WHOA!
TWK
IT'S SOUBI.
DAMN, HE GOT THE JUMP ON ME.
EEEEN
I DIDN'T EVEN SENSE HIS PRESENCE... DAMMIT!!

I...
...RELEASED THE BARRIER. THEY'LL BE HERE SOON.
THE ENEMY.
EEEEE
VWEEEE

SWSH
SO IT'S SEPTIMAL MOON? THE ONES WHO KILLED SEIMEI?!
"ENEMY" ...

GINKA.
OVER HERE.
ROGER.

RIGHT.
HOW DO YOU WANT ME TO HANDLE THEM, RITSUKA? WANT TO KILL THEM?

RSSH
WE'VE FOUND YOU, SOUBI!!
AND RITSUKA AOYAGI !!

LET'S FIGHT!
SWOSH
I ACCEPT.

THAT'S NOT IT.
BDMP
BDMP
I...
HOW DO YOU WANT ME TO HANDLE THEM, RITSUKA?
HERE.
FWIP
INSIDE THIS ENVELOPE IS THE INFORMATION YOU WANT, RITSUKA.
DO YOU WANT TO KILL THEM?

I WANT TO KNOW THE TRUTH.
IF YOU WIN, IT'S YOURS.
SYSTEMS ...
...EXPAND!

SOUBI.
THEIR ...
SKWEEZ
THE GIRL IS THE SACRIFICE.
WE WILL BE ON AUTOMATIC.
SWSH
EXPAND.
OH MY.
RIP
THEN I'LL TRY TO SPARE YOUR FACE.
I'VE NEVER HAD A MARK LEFT ON ME.
HA! DON'T WORRY.
I'M UP AGAINST A GIRL.

HMPH
BUT I APOLOGIZE IF MY AIM GOES ASTRAY.
LIGHTNING.
LIKE TEN MILLION ARROWS.
STRIKE WITH THE SPEED OF THE WIND!
GRAAA

THOK
THOK
THOK
THOK
WAH!
RESPOND ...
KIN!
RESPOND.
HE'S FAST.
THERE'S ONLY A SPLIT SECOND DELAY BETWEEN THE CASTING AND DEPLOYMENT OF THE SPELL.
I MADE SURE NOT TO STRIKE YOUR FACE.
DRIP

IF IT'S BETWEEN ME AND THAT LITTLE KID, I CAN TAKE WAY MORE PAIN.
WE JUST NEED TO CRUSH THE BRAT.
NOW IT'S OUR TURN.
USE A FULL POWER ATTACK.
EVEN IF SOUBI CAN HANDLE IT...
...THERE'S NO WAY THE KID CAN!
HE HASN'T GOTTEN SERIOUS YET...
SHOULDN'T WE BE ON DEFENSE ?
SKWEEZ
RITSUKA.
COMMAND ME!!

I...
I WANT THAT ENVELOPE!
GRRK
LICK
Um. Was that wrong?
I WANT TO FIND OUT WHY SEIMEI WAS KILLED.
DEFEAT THEM!!
WWE
TWO BEINGS WITH ONE NAME.
OUR NAME...
...IS SLEEP-LESS.

WITNESS ...
...THE DARK-NESS...
...OF A SLEEP-LESS NIGHT!
FWAAA
HAGRO
JANGLE
!!
SHANK
CHANG
BDMP
BDMP

WE DID IT!
HA HA!
WE RE-STRICTED HIM.
GR
GRRT

PAT
What is this?
...
I feel sick.
IT'S ONLY ...
...A SHAL-LOW DARK-NESS.
I'M FINE...
RITSUKA. ARE YOU ALL RIGHT ...?
INTER-CEDE.
INTER-FERE.
COME, STARS !!

SOUBI'S VOICE...
CUT OPEN THE DARKNESS AND FILL THE SKY WITH STARS.
PIXELS OF SPARKLING LIGHT...
...DEFY...
...THE NIGHT.
SOMETHING HURTS... AM I LOSING BLOOD? SUFFOCATING?
LIGHT...
...ENTERS.
IT INVADES.
THE STARS ARE FIRM IN THE FIRMAMENT.
HIS VOICE IS COMFORTING.

HIS WARM, DRY HANDS...
KIN! TURN OFF THE STARS.
I WANT BLACK CLOUDS.
IT FEELS NICE WHEN SOUBI TOUCHES ME.

THICK, DARK CLOUDS.
BLACK CLOUDS BLOCK ALL LIGHT.
ERASE THE STARS AND TRAP OUR ENEMY ...
...IN JET BLACK ...
DEEP, DARK CLOUDS FULL OF...
...LIGHT-NING AND ELECT-RICITY.
BECOME A VICIOUS THUNDER-STORM...

COME, DARK-NESS.
HE'S NOT JUST FAST...
CONCEAL EVERYTHING!
HE'S USING OUR OWN SPELLS AGAINST US!
...AND PUNCTURE THE DARKNESS.

PENE-TRATE.
COME, LIGHT.
PENE-TRATE EVERY-THING
!!
NOT ONE WORD ...
...OF DEFENSE ?
NGH...!
SHAA
WOO

BSHANG
THIS IS BAD.
THE MOMENTUM'S IN THEIR FAVOR.
DEFEND ...
SHIELD US...
...FROM THE ENEMY'S EYES...
...IN A PITCH BLACK ...
... CURTAIN OF DARKNESS.
ISN'T SOUBI HURTING TOO...?
OH... HE'S BLEEDING!!
JANGLE
FLAMES.

SLICE THROUGH THE DARKNESS.
TEAR EVERYTHING ASUNDER!
ENVELOP THEM WITH SCORCHING PAIN.
BURN BRIGHT, HELLFIRE.
WHATEVER PAIN I'M FEELING ...
HGCK!
!!
...I'M SURE THAT SOUBI IS SUFFERING MORE.

YOUR METHODS ARE WRONG!
YOU PISS ME OFF!
ALL YOU'RE DOING IS COASTING ON THE BACKS OF OUR SPELLS!
IF YOU BRING DARKNESS, I BRING STARS.
IF YOU BRING CLOUDS, I BRING RAIN.
IF YOU BRING A SHROUD, I BRING A FUNERAL PYRE.
TO TURN AN OPPONENT'S POWER BACK AGAINST THEM...
THAT'S ELEMENTARY.
I'M SICK OF YOU!
OOH, THE MODEL STUDENT!
I CAN SEE WHY YOU WERE THE PRINCIPAL'S PET. YOU PLAY DIRTY.
TWITCH
HE REACTED?! BUT TO WHAT?
TO "PRINCIPAL"?
TO "PET"?
TO "MODEL STUDENT"?
TO "DIRTY"?
TO WHAT?

NO, IT WAS TO "PRINCIPAL."
THE PRINCIPAL...
HE TAUGHT ME YOUR WEAKNESS.
SO IT'S TO "PET" ?!
HE ONLY PRAISED ME OUT OF NARCISSISM.
EVERYONE ...
...RECEIVED THE SAME INSTRUCTION.
WHO'D HAVE THOUGHT SAYING THAT WOULD PROVIDE AN OPENING?!
RESTRICT !!
YOU CAN NO LONGER MOVE!

SHANK
!!
JANGLE.
THAT'S RATHER...
...UN-PLEASANT.
BLACKNESS CRUSHES YOUR BODY AND SOUL.
DENY FREEDOM!
RE-STRICT!
RE-STRICT!
HAA...
SKWEE
I'M SORRY. ARE YOU IN PAIN ...?
YOUR HEART'S BEATING SO FAST.
SOUBI.
YOU CAN DO IT...
NGH...

I WANT THAT ENVELOPE NO MATTER WHAT.
GRR
TWK
GO GET IT!!
DON'T LOSE ...
YES...
...MASTER.

TOY'S MASTER / VOLUME OF THE ABSOLUTE TOY MASTER

CHAPTER 3

A NIGHT WITHOUT SLEEP.
THE ENEMY'S NAME IS SLEEPLESS.
WE DID IT!!
WE'VE RESTRICTED THEM!!
THIS IS LAUGH-ABLE.
HOW PATHETIC.
I SEE THROUGH YOUR SLEEPLESS NIGHT.

ABSOLUTE.
THAT ENVE-LOPE.
GO GET IT!
YES...
MASTER.
I SHALL ATTACK.
I WON'T REMOVE THEM.
THERE'S NO NEED.
GOT IT.
WHEN HE GOES TO REMOVE THE BONDS, THAT'S OUR CHANCE TO STRIKE.
KIN! IT'S OUR TURN.
SHAA

THAT WITHOUT EQUAL.
THAT WHICH OPPRESSES EVERY-THING.
OR...
I CAN'T MOVE. IS THIS WHAT "RESTRICTION" MEANS?
GRRK
FLAMES.
ROARING FLAMES.
I SHALL ATTACK WITH ABSOLUTE POWER.
...SOUBI'S STRONG ARMS AROUND ME?
...IS IT JUST...

RAZE.
!!
BACHANG
EEE!
BWASH
VWO
GYAAH!!

PCHING

YOU BASTARD!

I CAN'T STAND YOU!!
WHA...

WHAT ARE YOU DOING?!
BACK OFF!
ZSH

WHUMP
Ack!
SHOOF
IF YOU WANT TO SLUG IT OUT ...
...I'M FINE WITH THAT TOO.
OOF.
FWUMP
KIN!
HOLD ON!
NO FIGHT LEFT?
YANK
EEEEP! EEEEP!
ENOUGH ALREADY, SOUBI!

RITSUKA.
YOU HAVE TO KICK THEM WHEN THEY'RE DOWN.
NO, YOU DON'T!
Jerk!
Jerk!

WHAT WILL I...

...UH...

HERE.

THAT'S WHAT YOU HAVE THERE, RITSUKA.

FREEDOM.
...FIND INSIDE?

CHOICE.
THAT'S WHAT...
...YOU MUST MAKE, RITSUKA.
THE LAWS OF THE WORLD...
...HAVE DISINTE-GRATED BETWEEN YOU AND ME.
YOU ARE MY LAW, RITSUKA.
MY REASON FOR LIVING...
I AM YOUR FIGHTER.
USE ME AS YOU SEE FIT.
COMMAND ME.
DO IT AS YOU WISH.
WE ARE...
...IS YOU ALONE.

HE...
...WHO IS TO BE COMMANDED.
AND HE WHO COMMANDS.
...
IS THAT ALL WE ARE?
NEVER MIND.

RITSUKA?
TWIRL
IT'S NOTHING.

ARE YOU ANGRY, RITSUKA?
I'M NOT MAD!
WHO SAYS I'M MAD?!
RIP

W098N074A11T0005

WHAT DOES THIS HAVE TO DO WITH SEIMEI?
DOOM
WHAT...?
THIS IS IT?
WHAT THE...
N074A
LETTERS AND NUMBERS... I GUESS.
MAYBE A CODE?
HISS
HISS
HISS
HISS
AW, MAAAN!
SIGH...
...
...
OKAY...

dead serious

not so serious

I'M SORRY. IT'S MORE IMPORTANT ...
KLAK
KLAK
...THAT I TAKE CARE OF YOU, SOUBI!
BUT I'M FINE.
NO, YOU'RE NOT. I'M GOING TO TREAT THAT CUT.
OH.
WHY IS THIS ...
...BLEEDING?
BECAUSE I'M GOING AGAINST MY NAME.
OH...
UH...
I DON'T WANT TO TALK ABOUT IT.
HUH?
HMPH!
I DON'T WANT TO SPEAK OF IT.
HEY...
COME TO THINK OF IT ...
THAT GUY MENTIONED A PRINCIPAL.

SUDDENLY I REALIZED...

INSTEAD OF BEING TOLD TO "COMMAND HIM" OR HEARING THAT HE WOULD "DO ANYTHING I SAY"...

...THIS MADE ME HAPPIER.

THEN...

...DO AS YOU PLEASE.

I WANT SOME-THING REAL.

AFTER ALL...

...I...

EVEN IF YOU COMMAND ME, I WON'T DO IT.
That's an order!
WHA— WHY ?!
D-DUM
WHY NOT ?!
I wanna know!
That's not the deal!

THERE'S NO NOW OR LATER.
IT'S OKAY. I WON'T ASK RIGHT NOW.

YOU'RE SO FEISTY, RITSUKA.
4A11T0005

WELL FINE, THEN! GO HOME!
WHAP
THIS CODE IS YOUR HOMEWORK!! THINK ABOUT IT LONG AND HARD!

Ban!
GOOD NIGHT.
SWSSH
RSSSH
RSSSH
OH! LOOKS LIKE YOU FAILED AFTER ALL.
NGH...
WOBL...
KIN...
LET'S GO HOME.

SHA
YO!!
SHASHA
!!
IT'S YOU!!
WHAT'S ...
... WITH THAT BLOOD?
YOU DID SOME-THING BAD AGAIN...
YOU DIDN'T WIN, DID YOU?
AGAINST SOUBI ?
WE DON'T LIKE BAD LITTLE DOGS LIKE THAT.
WE DON'T LIKE YAPPY LITTLE DOGS.
OR WHIPPED DOGS.
Hee hee!
NO, WE DON'T ...
Hee!
!!

ドンッ!

SIGH
BLUB

BLUB
...tired.
Hm...
POKE

STARE
PLIP

K-TOMP
AN EMAIL ?!
SSH
BEEEP
BEEEP
BEEEP
SSH
0928soubi@docomo.n
e.jp
I forgot.
BDMP
BDMP
BDMP
BDMP
I forgot.
To Ritsuka
Kiss me.
BADUMP
e.jp
I forgot.
To Ritsuka
BIP
BIP

"KISS ME."
"I FORGOT."
SHAKE
SHAKE
SHAKE
HUH?!
"RITSUKA."
WHAT'S IT MEAN? WHAT AM I SUPPOSED TO DO?
PEEK
PEEK
K...
KISS ?!
PLIP...
IS HE SOME KIND OF IDIOT...?
Inbox
0928scout@docomo.ne.jp
I forgot.
To Ritsuka
Kiss me.
...
SPLISH

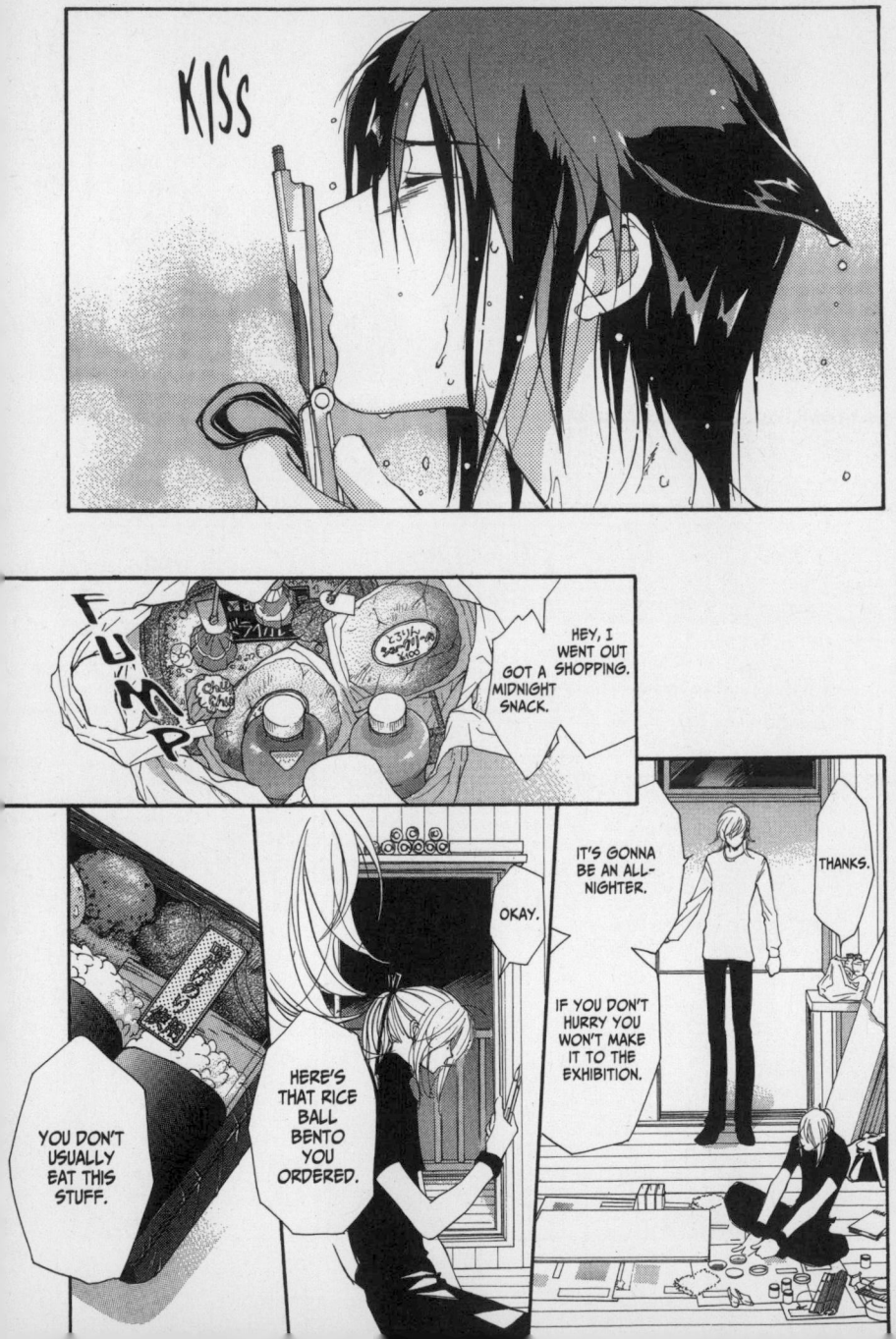
KISS
FUMP
HEY, I WENT OUT SHOPPING. GOT A MIDNIGHT SNACK.
THANKS.
IT'S GONNA BE AN ALL-NIGHTER.
IF YOU DON'T HURRY YOU WON'T MAKE IT TO THE EXHIBITION.
OKAY.
HERE'S THAT RICE BALL BENTO YOU ORDERED.
YOU DON'T USUALLY EAT THIS STUFF.

HEY, SOU...
... YOU'VE ... CHANGED, HAVEN'T YOU?
IT ACTUALLY LOOKS PRETTY GOOD.
IT'S THE BEST!
HUH.
I'M CURIOUS HOW THEY TASTE.
!
SOU !!
OH, AN EMAIL.
THIS IS A SERIOUS CONVERSATION HERE!
UH-HUH. FOR SURE!
PWEEP
YOU THINK?
PWEEP
PWEEP
BECAUSE OF THAT KID OR SOMETHING.
AGH!
ERK!
HEH HEH
WHAT THE HELL?
YOU PERV!

LET ME SEE! SHOW ME!!
A SEXY EMAIL?! FROM WHO?
WHAT, WHAT?! GROSS!
CHAK
You freak-show!
What are you saying?
I can't stand this anymore!
NOPE.

YUP.
I'M GETTING HARD.

BAM
BAM
BAM
HEY!!
WHY, YOU!
HEY!

HEE!

Hurry up and go to sleep!
Mwa
21ritsuka@doco
o.ne.jp
To Soubi
Hurry up and go to sleep!
SUB MENU
BACK
THANK YOU, RITSUKA.
"MWA."
LIKE A LITTLE MOUSE.
"MWA"...
...IT SAYS.
...
...
I'M NOT SURE THAT WAS THE BEST IDEA...
WAS THAT A MISTAKE ?
HMMMM.
FLICK

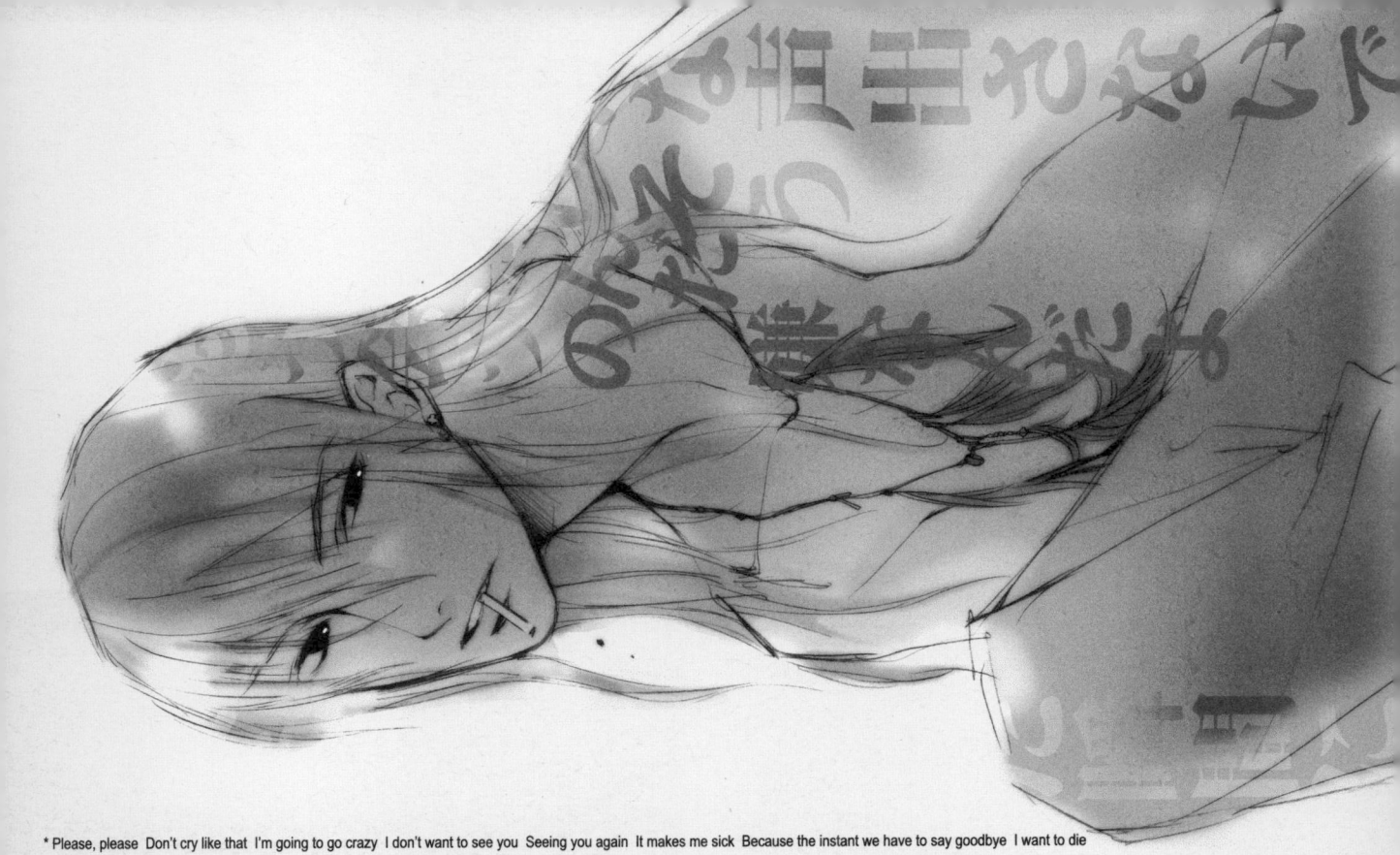

* Please, please Don't cry like that I'm going to go crazy I don't want to see you Seeing you again It makes me sick Because the instant we have to say goodbye I want to die

* Once I desire something I can't restrain myself Restraint
It's impossible for me I desire it Until it becomes mine
But there is no end No matter how much I take for myself

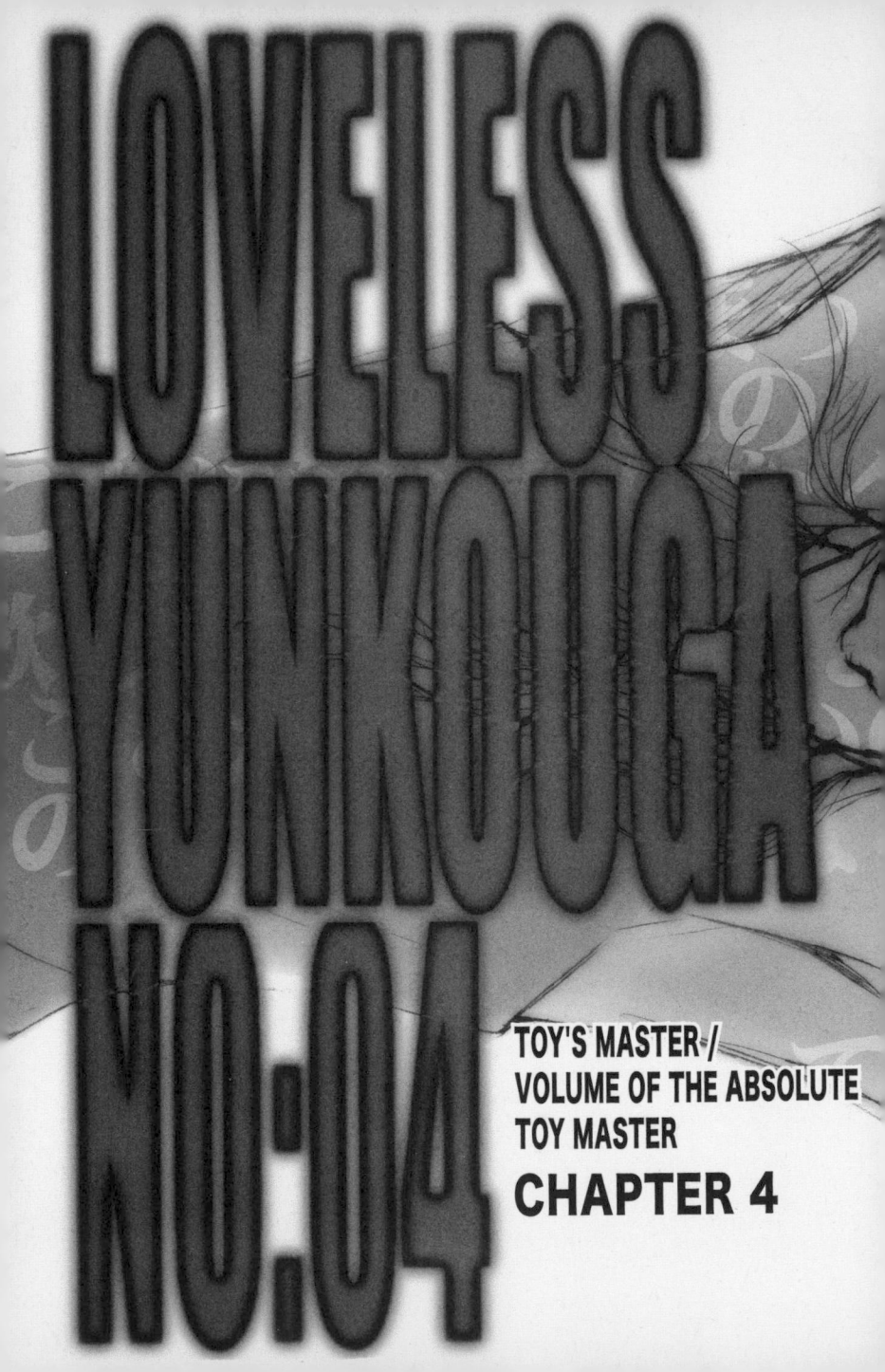

TOY'S MASTER /
VOLUME OF THE ABSOLUTE
TOY MASTER

CHAPTER 4

What a lame conversation.

RITSUKA, WANT TO JOIN THE ARTS AND CRAFTS CLUB?

ARTS AND CRAFTS...? DUNNO ABOUT THAT...
I MEAN, I CAN'T REALLY DRAW AND ALL.
ERGH
IT'S NOT REALLY ABOUT DRAWING.
ACTUALLY I'M JUST NOT VERY GOOD WITH MY HANDS.

OOH, THE ORCHESTRA! THAT SOUNDS FUN! ♡
...I DON'T WANT ANYTHING TOO INVOLVED.
LIKE I SAID...
NOBODY KNOWS HOW TO PLAY WHEN THEY START!!
KA
CHAK
THEN HOW ABOUT THE ORCHESTRA ?!
RIGHT NOW WE'RE LOOKING FOR ACCORDION PLAYERS!!
NO, I WANT RITSUKA TO...
THE ARTS AND CRAFTS CLUB IS ALL GIRLS TOO.
WHAT'S WRONG WITH THAT? IT'S EXTRA FUN WITH SO MANY GIRLS.
ANYWAY...
I'M THEIR FACULTY ADVISOR, YOU KNOW.
THEN HOW ABOUT THE ENGLISH CLUB?
UH.
BUT MS. SHINONOME, THE ENGLISH CLUB IS ALL GIRLS, ISN'T IT?!

WEDNESDAYS ...

...AREN'T GOOD FOR ME.

"I HAVE TO GO TO THE HOSPITAL EVERY WEEK."

I'VE ALWAYS SAID IT LIKE THAT, AND THEN KEPT MY DISTANCE FROM EVERYONE.

BUT TODAY THOSE WORDS WOULDN'T COME OUT.

ALWAYS THE SAME CONVERSATION.
DID ANYTHING INTERESTING HAPPEN THIS WEEK?
NOT REALLY ...
HOW ARE YOU, RITSUKA?
IT'S BEEN A WEEK.
DOING WELL?
FINE, I GUESS.
THAT HAS NEVER...
I really hate this
...HAPPENED BEFORE.
Y'KNOW, TODAY...
...INSTEAD OF ANSWERING MY QUESTIONS, WHY DON'T YOU JUST TALK, RITSUKA?

HUH...?

I'D LIKE TO HEAR WHAT YOU HAVE TO SAY.
YOU SEEM LIKE YOU'RE IN A GOOD MOOD TODAY.
THE SUBJECT DOESN'T MATTER, JUST TALK ABOUT ANYTHING.

THEN...
DR. KATSUKO ...
HM?
ARE YOU A PICKY EATER?

"RITSUKA" ALWAYS ATE A LOT OF JUNK.
AND MOM IS HUNG UP ON THAT, SO I CAN'T ASK HER TO CHANGE IT.
I MEAN, IT DOESN'T REALLY MATTER TO ME EITHER WAY.
BUT LATELY...

HOW LOVELY!
WHO DID YOU EAT WITH?

AND I THOUGHT THEY WERE REALLY GOOD.
IT SURPRISED ME.

... I'VE BEEN TRYING MORE THINGS.
I ATE FERMENTED SOYBEANS.
AND TOFU AND ASPARAGUS.

STARE
WITH...
WITH A FRIEND ...
RITSUKA.
YOU ARE A NORMAL PERSON.
AND YOU'RE A WONDERFUL BOY.
SMILE
YOUR MOTHER, AND MAYBE EVEN YOU, YOURSELF, CAN'T QUITE ACCEPT THIS...
BUT I KNOW.

I LIKE YOU A LOT, RITSUKA.
...
YOU LIKE ...
...ME ?
I DON'T KNOW WHY. I SHOULD BE HAPPY.
BUT I DON'T LIKE TO BE TOLD THAT.
I'M SORRY.
WHY IS THAT?
DR. KATSUKO.
SOMEONE SAYS "I LIKE YOU," (NOT THAT I HEAR IT OFTEN)...
...AND MY HEART GOES COLD.

WHETHER A CLASSMATE SAYS IT TO ME...
OR THE LUNCH LADY SAYS IT TO ME...
I ALWAYS THINK TO MYSELF...
"WHAT ON EARTH DO THEY MEAN?"

I LOVE YOU.
RITSUKA.
WHEN SOUBI SAYS THAT TO ME...
...IT ONLY HURTS.
SOUBI.

I THINK ABOUT LIFE A LOT.
DR. KATSUKO ...
I...

IF ONLY SEIMEI DIDN'T DIE.
...”IF ONLY MY LIFE COULD GO BACK TO THE WAY IT WAS.”
I ALWAYS THINK...

THAT'S REALLY WHAT I THINK ABOUT.
IF ONLY RITSUKA HADN'T DISAPPEARED.

I DON'T WANT TO MOVE ON.
BUT IF ONLY THE REST WOULD GO BACK TO THE WAY IT WAS.
I KNOW THAT I CAN'T DO ANYTHING ABOUT SEIMEI.

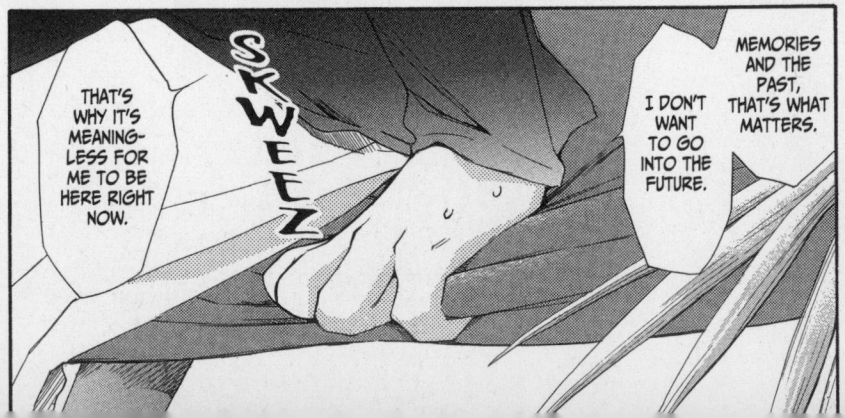
SKWEEZ
THAT'S WHY IT'S MEANING-LESS FOR ME TO BE HERE RIGHT NOW.
I DON'T WANT TO GO INTO THE FUTURE.
MEMORIES AND THE PAST, THAT'S WHAT MATTERS.

WHEN EVERYTHING GOES BACK TO THE WAY IT WAS...
...I'LL PROBABLY DISAPPEAR.
IT'S MEANINGLESS FOR ME TO BE HERE, BECAUSE I'M ONLY GOING TO DISAPPEAR.
YOU'RE NOT THE ONLY ONE WHO IS GOING TO EVENTUALLY DISAPPEAR, RITSUKA.
DON'T YOU THINK SO?
...IS ABOUT TRYING HARD UP UNTIL YOU DISAPPEAR.
BUT LIFE...
ONE DAY, EVERYONE DISAPPEARS.

THEN...
MAYBE NOBODY KNOWS?
WHY WERE WE BORN?
THAT'S RIGHT.
WHY DO WE LIVE?
THAT'S NOT FAIR.
WHY DO WE DIE?
I THOUGHT THAT ADULTS WOULD KNOW.

CHAK
GOOD WORK. I'LL SEE YOU NEXT WEEK.
THANK YOU VERY MUCH.
HEY...
RITSUKA?
THAT SCRAPE. YOUR MOTHER REALLY DIDN'T DO THAT?
I'M WORRIED ABOUT YOU...
I'LL SEE YOU...
...NEXT WEEK!!
WHAP

WHY ARE YOU IN SUCH A BAD MOOD...
...DR. KATSUKO ?
IT'S NOTHING.
I JUST CAN'T FIGURE OUT WHAT HIS MOTHER WANTS.
WHAT DOES SHE WANT FROM RITSUKA?!
SIGH

YOU SHOULDN'T GET SO PERSONALLY INVOLVED.
ERK ...!
BUT...! RITSUKA IS REALLY...

IF I WERE 20 YEARS YOUNGER I'D MAKE A MOVE ON HIM.
OH STOP THAT, DOCTOR.
DR. KATSUKO, YOU HAVE A GUEST.

I DON'T HAVE ANY APPOINTMENTS SCHEDULED.
ME?
IT'S THE POLICE.
THE POLICE...
UH...
IT'S ABOUT RITSUKA AOYAGI...
HMM...
THEN, I'LL ALSO TAKE...
...THREE CHESTNUT KANOKO.
TAK
TAK
MAYBE I...
...SHOULDN'T HAVE BROUGHT A GIFT AFTER ALL.
URH...
Thank you very much!
KINAKO MOCHI

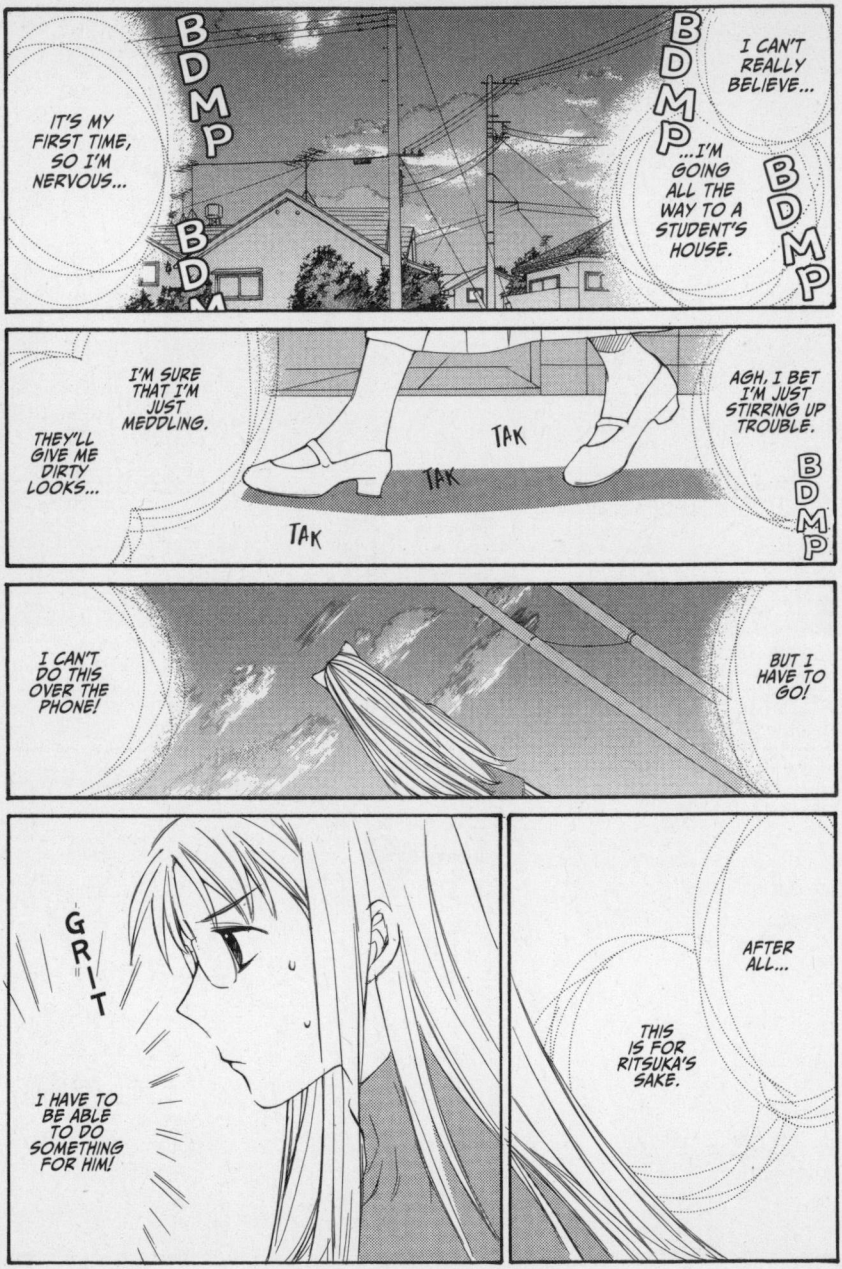
IT'S MY FIRST TIME, SO I'M NERVOUS...
BDMP
BDMP
I CAN'T REALLY BELIEVE...
...I'M GOING ALL THE WAY TO A STUDENT'S HOUSE.
BDMP
THEY'LL GIVE ME DIRTY LOOKS...
I'M SURE THAT I'M JUST MEDDLING.
TAK
TAK
TAK
AGH. I BET I'M JUST STIRRING UP TROUBLE.
BDMP
I CAN'T DO THIS OVER THE PHONE!
BUT I HAVE TO GO!
GRIT
I HAVE TO BE ABLE TO DO SOMETHING FOR HIM!
AFTER ALL...
THIS IS FOR RITSUKA'S SAKE.

HEY, LADY.
ARE YOU FROM AROUND HERE?
DO YOU KNOW WHERE THE AOYAGI HOUSE IS?
KRCH
WELL?
HUH... AH...
WHEN YOU SAY AOYAGI, DO YOU MEAN...
RITSUKA AOYAGI'S HOUSE.
YOU'RE LOOKING FOR RITSUKA'S HOUSE?
ARE YOU HIS FRIENDS?
FRIENDS?
HEH
HEH
HEH

HEH
YOU HAVE YOUR EARS.
HEH
HEY LADY, ARE YOU A VIRGIN?
EVEN THOUGH YOU'RE AN ADULT?
THAT'S SO WEIRD!
OKAY...
WHAT'S GOING ON? ARE THEY FROM HIS OLD SCHOOL?
WELL, THEN.
LET'S GO, LET'S GO.
IF YOU KNOW, THEN SHOW US THE WAY.
BLUSH
IT...
IT ISN'T WEIRD.
I LIKE IT THIS WAY!
THAT'S JUST ME, GOING AT MY OWN PACE!

OH REALLY.
BUT NORMALLY ...
HEH
Y'KNOW ?
HEH
...BY THE TIME SOMEONE'S AN ADULT THEY'VE ALREADY HAD SEX...
...AND LOST THEIR EARS.
OH REALLY ...?
YOU'RE...
HEH
HEH
HEH
...
PRETTY FUNNY.
YUP.
YOU SURE ARE FUNNY.
THAT MAY BE TRUE!
BUT EVERY-ONE HAS TO DO WHAT'S RIGHT FOR THEM.
I THINK THAT I'M FINE THE WAY I AM!

WHA...
WHAT THE?!
HA!
CUTE, SHE SAYS!!
HEE
HEE
HEE
FUNNY...
YOU THINK SO?
WELL, I THINK YOU TWO...
...ARE VERY CUTE.
HEH
I...
HEH
HEH
I LIKE HER.
YEAH, I LIKE HER TOO.
I...
...DON'T GO FOR OLDER WOMEN.

BLUSH
GOSH.
THE LAST TIME I CAME, MR. AGATSUMA WAS HERE...
HEY!! HE'S YOUNGER THAN ME.
I'M OLDER THAN HIM! BUT HE PROBABLY THINKS I'M SOME OLD MAID!
WHY AM I BOTHERING WITH THE "MR."?!
WHY DID I REMEMBER THAT, OF ALL THINGS?!
...I'LL DROP THE "MR."!
THE NEXT TIME I SEE HIM...
GRIND GRIND GRIND
GRIND GRIND
THAT STUPID AGATSUMA !!
HEY...
TELL US YOUR NAME.

HUH?
HEY, C'MON.
YOUR NAME.
OH, I'M SORRY.
I'M SHINO-NOME.
YOUR FIRST NAME.
WHAT ABOUT THAT?
HITOMI.
I'M HITOMI SHINO-NOME.
HMM.
HEE
HEE
THAT'S CUTE.
"HITOMI."
HITOMI.
SKWEEZ
...?

I SHALL CONTROL ...
...THAT NAME.

SHE IS OUR PREY.
ENSLAVE.
?!
PTCH
DSTAAA
HITOMI IS OURS.
WE HAVE CAPTURED HITOMI.
MY LEGS...
...WON'T MOVE?
Y'SEE, WE WERE THINKING ...
...THAT IT WAS ABOUT TIME WE GOT RID OF OUR EARS.
HITOMI.
ALL RIGHT.

TOY'S MASTER / VOLUME OF THE ABSOLUTE TOY MASTER
CHAPTER 5

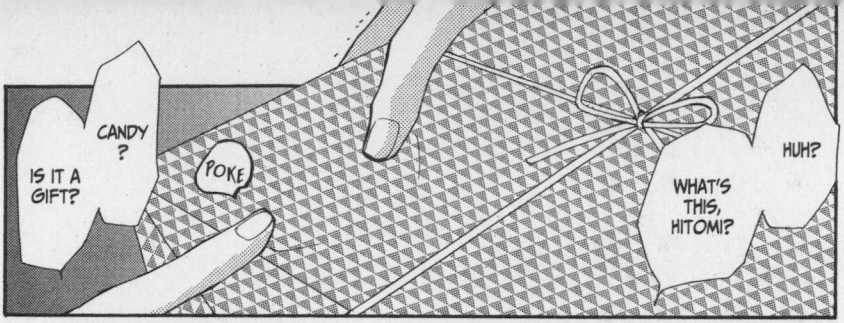
HUH?
WHAT'S THIS, HITOMI?
POKE
CANDY ?
IS IT A GIFT?

WERE YOU GOING SOME-WHERE ?
WHERE ?
I WONDER IF THERE'S A GOOD PLACE FOR IT AROUND HERE?
I DUNNO ...
Hmm...

WHA... WHAT... WHY?
MY BODY...
I CAN'T CONTROL IT AT ALL...
WHAT'S WRONG ?
HITOMI?

COME ON.
...
NO...
YOU AREN'T GETTING AWAY.
WHAT...
...DID YOU DO TO ME...

I SAW ONE WHEN WE GOT HERE.
WHERE SHOULD WE GO?
LET'S GO. LET'S GO.
THE PARK. IT'S GOTTA BE THE PARK.

COME ON.
COME ON, WALK WITH YOUR OWN TWO FEET...
HITOMI.

CALL ME MS. SHINONOME! WE'VE ONLY JUST MET!
WOW, YOU REALLY DON'T KNOW THE POSITION YOU'RE IN, HITOMI.
G
RA

...YOU TALK TO YOUR ELDERS.
THAT ...
THAT'S NOT HOW...
STOMP
STOMP

I...
...DON'T KNOW...
...WHAT YOU DID TO ME.
BUT I KNOW IT'S NOT FAIR.
FAIR?
WE DON'T LIKE FAIR.
THERE'S NO SUCH THING AS FAIR.

Sneak
IF I PRETEND I DIDN'T SEE AND JUST WALK AWAY, AND RITSUKA FINDS OUT LATER...
...HE'LL PROBABLY GET REALLY MAD.
WELL, WELL.
WE MEET AGAIN. WHAT A BOTHER.
...!! MR AGATSUMA ...
YOUJI.
AND YOU ...?
NATSUO.
STATE YOUR NAMES.

SOUBI AGATSUMA.
I'M LOVELESS'S FIGHTER.
DON'T BUTT IN, SOUBI AGAT-SUMA.
I'M AFRAID I WILL.
WHERE WERE YOU TAKING THIS WOMAN-CHILD?
MS. SHINO-NOME.
POKE
GO HOME.
Yeek!
SWF
TWITCH

BLUSH
IF I LEAVE YOU WITH THEM, RITSUKA WILL GET ANGRY.
DID HE JUST...
HUH?! WAIT A MINUTE.
...CALL ME A WOMAN-CHILD?
UH.
MR. AGA...
I MEAN, AGAT-SUMA.
YOU... YOU...
ARE YOU ALL RITSUKA'S FRIENDS?
HUH ?!
I MEAN ...
BLUSH
NO!
THAT'S NOT WHAT I MEANT TO SAY.

THIS IS NONE OF YOUR BUSI-NESS.
SLEEP.
MR. AGAT-SUMA ...
THIS IS NONE OF YOUR BUSINESS.
DO I REALLY ...
...SAY SUCH TERRIBLE THINGS?
WHY DO YOU ALWAYS ...
...SAY SUCH TERRIBLE THINGS...
WHAT A...
...MEAN THING TO SAY!
SLUMP
YOU DO...
THEN I'M SORRY.

GRR
GRR
GRR
GRR
GRR
GRR
YOU TWO KNOW EACH OTHER?
SHE BELONGS TO US.
YOU'RE PISSING US OFF.
GRR
GRR
GRR
GRR
GRR
GIVE HER BACK.
IF YOU DON'T, WE'LL KILL YOU.
THAT'S A REAL THREAT. WE'RE STRONG.
GRR
GRR
GRR
GRR
YOU DON'T EVEN KNOW OUR NAME, DO YOU?
WE'VE NEVER LOST TO ANYONE.
I THINK NOT.
ENOUGH TALK. SHOW ME WHAT YOU'VE GOT.

YOU'RE GONNA REGRET THAT.
WE'RE ...
...ZERO.
ZERO?!
THEY'RE ZEROES ?!
SYSTEMS EXPAND.
I ACCEPT.
DOMAIN SYSTEMS ...
EXPAND.
WE DECLARE BATTLE.
VWEEN

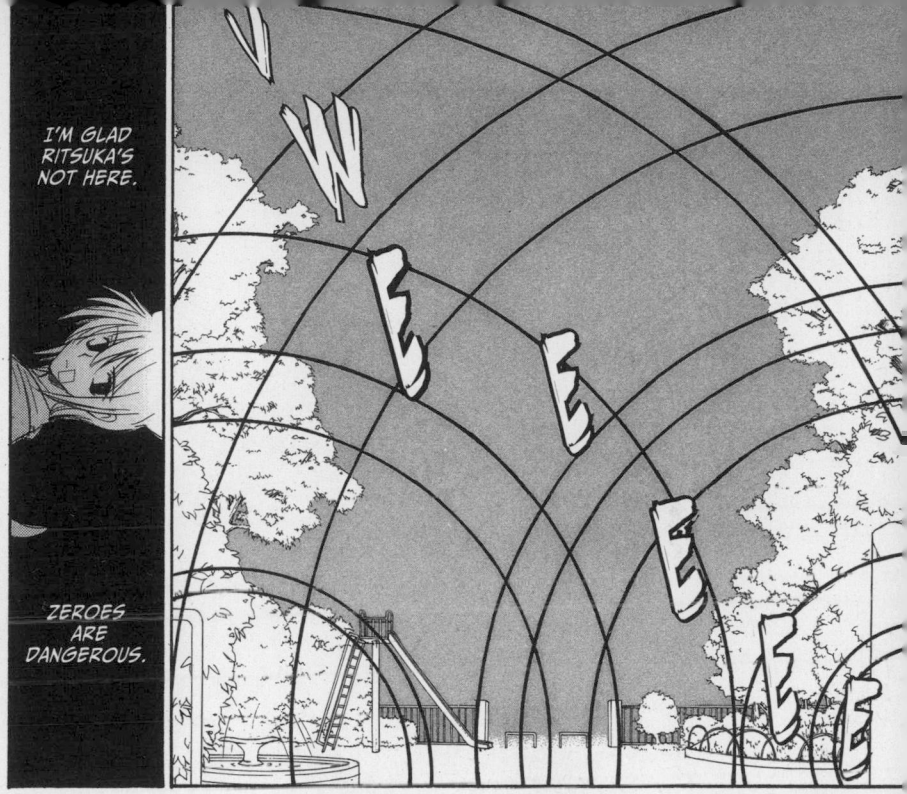
I'M GLAD RITSUKA'S NOT HERE.
ZEROES ARE DANGEROUS.
WEEEEE

RMMMMMM
IT'S TWO ON ONE, BUT WE'RE NOT GOING TO HOLD BACK.
AND YOU REALLY MADE US MAD, TOO.
YOU'RE GOING TO TAKE US ON BY YOURSELF?
YOU DON'T NEED LOVELESS?

WITH A DIFFERENT NAME, YOUR POWER IS HALVED.
AND WITHOUT A SACRIFICE, YOUR POWER IS HALVED AGAIN.
YOU STILL WANT TO TAKE US ON?
BE GENTLE WITH ME.
YOU REALLY ...
...PISS US OFF !!
SUPER PISSED!
WE'RE GOING TO TEAR YOU TO BITS.
Second District Park

ZZRT
ZZRT
ZZRT
WATCH OUT FOR THE...
...HIGH VOLTAGE CURRENT.
PSHAK
SHATTER.
OUR NAME IS ZERO.
WE ARE THE BEGINNING AND THE END.
WE ARE EVERY-THING.
AND NOTHING.

WE SHALL GIVE YOU PAIN AND SUFFERING.
WE SHALL REDUCE YOUR EXISTENCE TO NOTHING.
WHAT...
...A NICE PHRASE.
"REDUCE MY EXISTENCE TO NOTHING."
WAS IT?
HW
I LIKE THAT.
A LOT.

WOO
SHA
ZZRI
ZZRI

I SEE.
THEY'RE FAST...
CON-DENSE!
RE-LEASE!

I HEARD THAT YOU'VE GOT...
...A HIGH PAIN TOLERANCE.
RELEASE.
CONGEAL!
SOLIDIFY INTERNALLY.
DISSOLVE THESE BONDS.

I WONDER.
LET'S FIND OUT!
I DON'T THOUGH.
WOOO

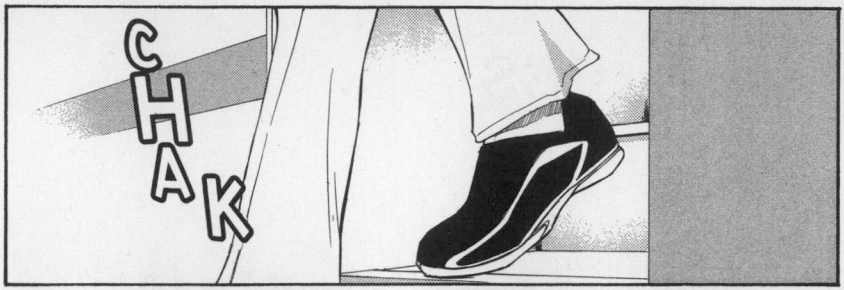
CHAK

AH.

VROOOOM
DR. KATSUKO INVITED ME ON A DATE THE OTHER DAY.
BUT...
WE HAVEN'T GONE YET.
I WANT TO GO. I WANT TO MAKE MORE MEMORIES.

MOTSU
TRC!

loveless
●IN THE SUMMER 1/2●
FOLLOW YOU

TODAY I'M STALKING A GRADE SCHOOLER.
REEE
...
REEE
REEE
HELLO. I'M KIO KAIDOU. (YEAH, I KNOW. IT'S A WEIRD NAME.)

OOPS, MY MISTAKE.
I'M JUST TAGGING ALONG WITH A PERVERT.
KIO.
YOU WANT A BEER?

AND I'D LIKE A TUNA SKEWER.
MAKE IT ICE COLD.
THIS GUY IS SOUBI AGATSUMA (AGE 20).

HE'S A TOTAL STALKER.
IT'LL BE A HASSLE IF WE LOSE THEM.
WERE YOU KEEPING AN EYE ON RITSUKA AND THE OTHERS?

THIS GUY IS A PEDO FREAK WHO'S OBSESSED WITH A SIXTH GRADER.
I'M WATCHING.
I THINK THEY'RE OVER THERE BUYING JUICE.
HE'S DITCHING ME.
HE WANTS TO MAKE MEMORIES WITH HIS FRIENDS.
JUST GO UP TO RITSUKA AOYAGI AND ASK TO PLAY WITH HIM.
SOU, WHY DON'T YOU STOP THIS?
I CAN'T THIS TIME.
LAST NIGHT HE WARNED ME OFF.
DO I REALLY HAVE NOTHING BETTER TO DO WITH MY SUMMER VACATION? ★
HMM...

BUT IF IT WEREN'T FOR THIS KIND OF THING...
...SOUBI WOULD BE A PRETTY FINE CATCH.

HE'S TALL, AND HIS LOOKS AREN'T BAD.
AND ABOVE ALL, HE'S A TALENTED ARTIST. IT'S STARTING TO GET ON MY NERVES, TO BE HONEST.

ON THE OTHER HAND...
IF IT WEREN'T FOR THIS, HE MIGHT AS WELL HAVE BEEN A WALKING CORPSE.

BEFORE HE MET RITSUKA AOYAGI...
...HE WAS LIKE A ZOMBIE.

AGH, NO WAY!!
I'M SCARED OF FERRIS WHEELS.
WHY?
THEY SHAKE!! YOU COULD FALL!!
OH.
YOKOHAMA

AAH.
LOOK.
LOOK, KIO.
THEY'RE GOING TO RIDE THE COSMO CLOCK.

LIAR.
THAT'S TRUE.
THAT LOOK IN YOUR EYES SAYS YOU'RE NOT AFRAID OF ANYTHING RIGHT NOW.
IT IS SCARY.
AHA.
HE'S CHECKING HIS EMAIL.
HEH
TOO BAD. I'M NOT SENDING YOU ANY TODAY.

BUT YOU SEE, KIO...
I'M WAITING. I'M NOT RUSHING THINGS.

IF YOU WANT TO GO TO HIM, GO.
YOU'RE SO STUBBORN.

YIKES, THAT'S YOUR GAME?
IS THAT SOMETHING YOU DO TO A GRADE SCHOOLER? YOU CREEP!
YOU'RE QUITE PECULIAR YOURSELF, KIO, TAGGING ALONG WITH ME.
WELL, EXCUSE ME!

I'LL MAKE MY MOVE AFTER RITSUKA GETS A GOOD TASTE...
...OF WHAT IT'S LIKE TO BE WITHOUT ME.

YOU'RE ...
...WELCOME.
NO, I APPRECIATE IT.
THANKS. YOU'RE MY BEST FRIEND.
WAAAH, THAT WAS SO SCARY!
HOW CAN YOU BE SCARED OF HEIGHTS WHEN YOU'RE SO TALL, YUIKO?
EVEN IF YOU'RE TALL, SCARY THINGS ARE SCARY.
...HUH?
HUH?! WHAT?!
What are you doing here?

loveless
Yawn
IN THE SUMMER 2/20
STAND BY ME?

WHAT I KNOW ABOUT HIM:
1. HE'S AT THE SAME SCHOOL AS ME, BUT IN A DIFFERENT CLASS.
2. HE'S SHORT.
3. HE HAS A GIRLY NAME.
AND...

(YOU'RE REALLY ONE TO TALK, I THOUGHT.)
HE'S IN LOVE WITH YUIKO.
YOU'RE PRETTY GIRLY, AREN'T YOU?

SUMMER'S ALMOST OVER.
I'M MAKING MEMORIES.
IT'S HOT.
I'VE NEVER BEEN TO YOKOHAMA BEFORE! OOH, THE OCEAN!
IT'S WAY CLOSER THAN I THOUGHT!
IT'S REALLY FAST WHEN YOU TAKE THE TOYOKO LINE.
YUIKO, YOU SHOULD WEAR A HAT.
I DON'T LIKE HATS. MY EARS GET SWEATY.
HEY, SOU. EVEN JUST STALKING GRADE SCHOOLERS ...
...IS STILL A CRIME.
YOU THINK ?
WELL...
...LAST NIGHT...

OKAY. WHERE ARE WE GOING?
I'M GOING OUT TOMORROW TO MAKE SOME MEMORIES.
WITHOUT YOU, SOUBI!
I CAN'T HAVE YOU ALWAYS HANGING AROUND ME.
I'M GOING TO YOKOHAMA WITH MY FRIENDS!
MEANING?
THAT'S NO WAY TO MAKE A COLLECTION!
ALL I HAVE ARE PICTURES WITH YOU.
YES, IT'S SO!!
HISS!
IS THAT SO?

WHAT?
WHAT IS IT?!
NOTH-ING.
THAT'S OKAY, YOU DON'T HAVE TO TAKE ME.
SMILE
IF IT'S OKAY, THEN DON'T SAY IT LIKE THAT.
RITSUKA...
YOU'RE STILL JUST A CHILD.
B-
BMP

...THE MORE YOU THINK ABOUT ME.
THAT THE MORE YOU SPEND TIME AWAY FROM ME...
YOU DON'T UNDERSTAND YET.

REEE
REEE
REE

WHAT'S WITH HIM?
I WAS SURE THAT HE WOULD SEND ME SOME WEIRD EMAIL...
...OR TRY TO MESS WITH ME.
GOT A MESSAGE?
UH, NO...
It's freaking me out.
STARE
SILENCE
IT'S HOT, ISN'T IT?!
I'LL GO GET SOME MOMI TEA!! SOME COLD ONES! ♡
WAIT HERE, GUYS!
EASIER SAID THAN DONE!!
YOU GUYS CAN PLAY. ♡
THAT'S OKAY, I'M FINE.
Lal
I'LL GO TOO, YUIKO!
H-HEY!

I WANT TO RIDE THE FERRIS WHEEL.
TODAY YAYOI CAME TOO.
I'M GONNA TRY TO MAKE THIS WORK!!
I HAVE TO TAKE LOTS OF PICTURES!
OOF!
OOF!
THREE OF THEM ?
GOT IT OKAY ?
ER, I'M FINE !!
RITSUKA'S MAKING MEMORIES.
I'LL DO ANYTHING...
HEEEY!
...IF IT'S FOR RITSUKA.
WHAT?
IT'S GOT SOFT CHEWY STUFF INSIDE.
DRINK UP!
YOU LIKE THAT, RIGHT, RITSUKA ?
HERE, MILK TEA FLA-VORED.
I DO.

HM?
HEY!
HE DRANK IT.
HEY, THIS ONE'S RED BEAN MILK.
That's mine.
WOW, THAT LOOKS GOOD.
YOU WANT A TASTE?
SURE.
?
I GUESS.
You can try it too.
SLRRRP
HUH?
UH ...
I MEAN ...
YOU GUYS GET ALONG WELL.
CLICK

KREE
KREE
KREE
KREE
...
...
...
W-WE'RE FINE. IF WE DO FALL, IT'LL BE OVER FAST.
WE COULD FALL?!
SWOOSH
...
What a lame conversation.
KREE
IT'S ROCKING!
DON'T WORRY! WE WON'T FALL!
KREE
KREE
IT...
IT REALLY...
YAYO! !
IT ROCKS A LOT MORE THAN I EXPECTED.
DON'T MOVE!
IT'S ROCKING.
KREE

KREE
I DIDN'T REALIZE IT WHEN I WAS LOOKING UP FROM THE GROUND ...
WOO
KREE
WOO
THE WIND'S REALLY STRONG WHEN YOU'RE HIGH IN THE SKY.
KREE
IT'S BEAUTIFUL.

I WISH...
...THAT SOUBI...
...COULD SEE IT.

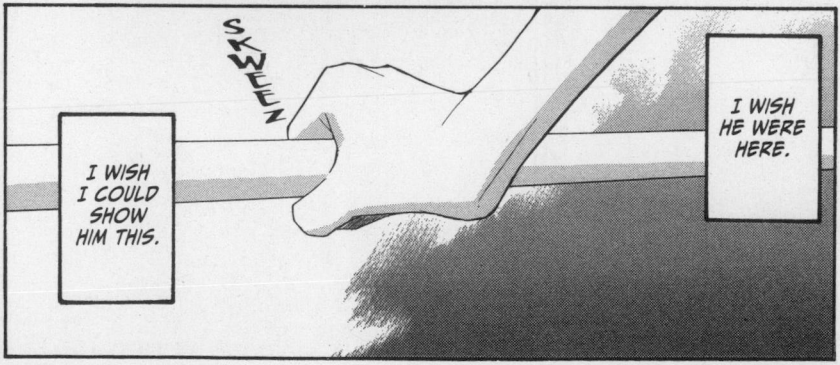
SKWEEN
I WISH I COULD SHOW HIM THIS.
I WISH HE WERE HERE.

I'M NOT THAT TALL!!
RITSUKA !!
How mean!
HUH.
HUH.
YOU'RE SO TALL, YUIKO, AND YOU'RE SCARED OF HEIGHTS?
WAH, THAT WAS SO SCARY!
NO MORE FERRIS WHEELS!
WHAT...
...ARE YOU DOING HERE?
NO WAY ...
EVEN IF YOU'RE TALL, SCARY THINGS ARE SCARY.
FLICK

DOING WELL, YUIKO?
OH, VERY AFRAID. ♡
IT'S SOUBI! HELLO! ARE YOU AFRAID OF HEIGHTS?! ♡
EEE! EEE!
YAY!
I'M GREAT!
WHAT A FAKER!
DIDN'T YOU CALL ME?
WHA...
OF COURSE NOT!!
NOTHING...
I CAN SEE IT IN YOUR EYES.
...SCARES YOU.

LET'S GO, RITSUKA.
TUG
HUH?
That's a...
...lie.
IT'S QUITE THE COIN-CIDENCE.
SMILE
WOW, WHAT ARE YOU DOING HERE?
YOU WANT TO RIDE ON THE FERRIS WHEEL, RIGHT?
WHAT A WEIRDO! WEIRDO!
THIS IS WHAT HE WANTED TO DO ?
LET'S GO AGAIN.
I did too!
I JUST GOT OFF IT...!

LOVELESS 2 / END

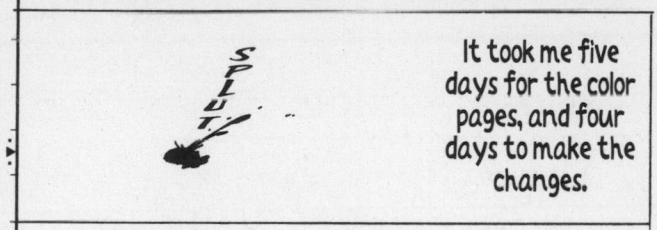

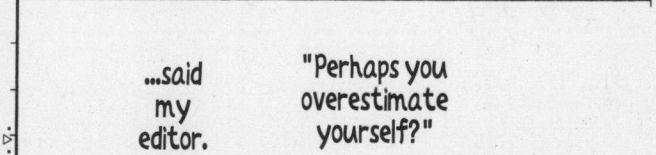

Loveless Afterword

This Just In!

Yun Kouga Near Death!

Ugh, I feel sick.

Come by and play! http://www.kokonoe.com

Here's the official website.

But they're just dreams. They don't mean anything.

...What happened next...

I wonder...

...

SILENCE

FUTON

Whaaat?!

Do you want to go to a hotel?

For example...

....

Thanks, Dream Soubi.

Or...

What's inside me?

There are nails and a hammer in me.

Or this.

SOMETHING AWFUL, I'M SURE

Sometimes I see them in my dreams.

But for some reason...

...in my dreams...

EEK!

WHY!!

I see things I can't tell anybody about.

It's been a year since I started drawing *Loveless*. And I think I've finally gotten used to Ritsuka and friends.

MEOW

RITSUKA

Well then, until volume 3, I bid you adieu!!

?

It says, "For Use by Yun Kouga" on it.

It makes me draw three times faster!!

Sieg Zeon!

By the way...

My manga paper is special order.

Isn't this convenient, it's an original!!

THIS

Now then, since I previously (in volume 1) made public my work paper, a certain group of my friends wanted some, so I've been sharing it around.

This has been *Loveless* volume 2. What's with me, drawing cat ears in this new millennium? But, come to think of it, *Zero-Sum* manga has an awful lot of cat ears. I put a lot of effort into drawing Ritsuka's ears. Since he's not very talkative, I have him express his feelings through his ears and tail. Kinda convenient things to have! (Although I think I'd pass on the tail—it'd hurt if I wound up sleeping on it!)

—*Yun Kouga, 2003*

loveless

(little loveless)

by Yun Kouga

Thank you for purchasing this special limited edition!! Off we go, into the world of loveless !!

Injured
and
Unloved
loveless

DOES A BODY GOOD♥

I think it's a convenient, drinkable product.

ABOUT CHRISTMAS

My Christmas was just full of work.

THE DEVIL'S NUMBER

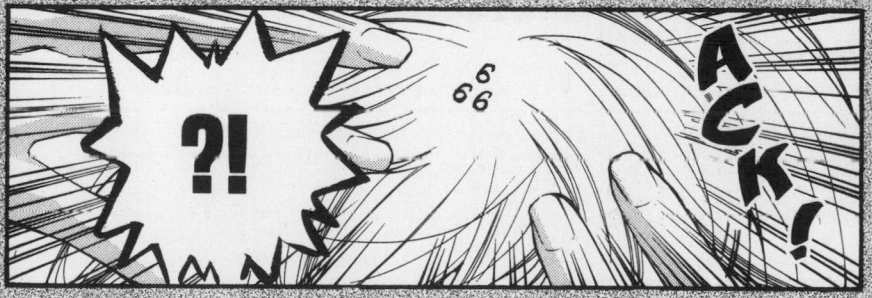

Not true.

Soubi is tainted, so ears don't suit him.

A Conversation, to the Ends, Sans Underwear, and with a Toothache (and too long a title) !!!!

Kouga: Good evening!! I'm sleepy, so I have no idea what I'm going to write!! I'm the manga artist!

Sugino: ...Good evening! I'm in pretty bad shape too. I'm the editor, currently on the verge of saying something I shouldn't to my artist...

Ⓚ: (gets insult deja vu) GIGGLE! This time we worked even harder than before!

Ⓢ: Well, it's definitely been "hard" in terms of keeping quality, making quantity, and sticking to schedule... Yes, I mean that in a bad way, and yes, forget I said that.

Ⓚ: (is the better man) Master Sugi said just now, "You think you maybe put too much energy into drawing Kio?"

Ⓢ: Kio's the one who's most like you, isn't he, Ms. Kouga? And I've heard you say, "If I had to date anybody, it would be Kio..." So does that mean...?

Ⓚ: Who said that?! You're making that up!

Ⓢ: Birds of a feather. "Caregiver" + "likes dirty jokes" + "obsession with Chupa Chups." You see?

Ⓚ: (Eeeek!!) (Cats are being stuffed into clothes...) In any case, volume 2 is incredible.

Ⓢ: Incredible? I guess so. It IS incredible. At least the number of self-portraits you've included is. How many are there?

Ⓚ: An 800% increase over normal. This time, you see, I fine-tuned it like never before. I'm totally satisfied with this one!

Ⓢ: That's wonderful. I hope the readers are happy too. By the way, is that pork miso soup?

Ⓚ: It's cold soup over rice! After that bread I ate, I went for soup. *MUNCH MUNCH*

Ⓢ: Eat lots and grow up big and strong! You do cook quite a bit while you work, don't you...

Ⓚ: *MUNCH MUNCH* My assistants do the cooking. Sorry, I'm so hungry that I've been eating and writing at the same time.

Ⓢ: And there's nothing to talk about! I mean, all I can think of are sketchy things!

Ⓚ: Please cheer up. Please don't sleep in your car. Don't eat sukiyaki bento at dawn.

Ⓢ: It doesn't matter what happens to my body. But...perhaps drinking four liters of juice a day is extreme. And...you just keep eating.

Ⓚ: Always munch-a-lunching (I didn't have time to eat a real meal). By the way, do you realize Ritsuka's not wearing any pants in that illustration spread?

Ⓢ: Oh god, it's true! And he's only a grade schooler! But I guess age doesn't matter. But everyone in "little [redacted] loveless" is really cute.

Oops

Ⓚ: No white-out... Please let me draw for little zero-sum as well! Ritsuka in little loveless seems to have a blushing problem.

Ⓢ: I'm sooorryyy (sob). Whatever happens, please keep hammering away and drawing your manga. Children blush a lot.

Ⓚ: People who blush easily are sexy, aren't they? It's like, what were you thinking just now?!

Ⓢ: But when KIDS blush it's because they're nervous! You just can't get your mind out of the gutter, can you? I bet you don't even blush.

Ⓚ: No, I don't. It's fine. Yes, it's fine. I've lost 5 kb. I made some tea. Drink it.

Ⓢ: You're fine? Uh...what's fine? By the way, what did you mean by "kb?" That's a mistake, right?

Ⓚ: (Can't you tell?!) ...hey, can I talk about...my tooth...really hurting.

Ⓢ: Your tooth?! That's terrible! Go to the doctor, or the hospital!! ...I mean, when you have the time. Yeah.

Ⓚ: Who are you trying to impress with that attitude? It'll be fine!! No toothache can win against my exhaustion!! Ha ha ha ha!!

Ⓢ: I worry about your pages. Why is Loveless always such an adventure? D:

Ⓚ: (It's like some strange musical instrument). It'll be fine!! Next time I'll draw Soubi without pants!! You'd think I was a pervert or something!

ROSY DAYS

by_Yutaka Kasami

Seimei told me that if he died, I was to go to Ritsuka. And Seimei died.

A master's orders are absolute. Disobedience is unthinkable; it cannot be done. When I heard these orders, as good as his last will and testament, I never dreamed they'd become reality. It was inconceivable, since a Fighter is almost always destroyed before a Sacrifice. But regardless of my own wishes, these prescient words became orders.

To Ritsuka I went.

These orders, a supreme honor for me, were simple in intent, but very difficult in execution. I operated under the assumption that Seimei wanted me to become Ritsuka's Fighter and thus protect him, because Seimei loved Ritsuka. A master's orders are absolute.

I agonized to death over how to best obey these orders. How would I approach Ritsuka? What if I barged into his house and announced that I was Seimei's Fighter? There were no indications that Seimei had told his family about himself. So naturally, the Aoyagi family, including Ritsuka, would not have been aware of my existence.

I decided Ritsuka would accept me more readily if I came into his life naturally. That would not include a proposition like, "Hey, little boy, you want to do something fun with me?" I'd be hauled off by the police.

As I was about to put my brush to Japanese paper, Kio called out to me.

"What do you want to do with this? Not like it has anything to do with you." *What a pain. If it doesn't have anything to do with me... Student teaching...?*

I grabbed the printouts from Kio's hands. According to the info from Seimei, Ritsuka was eleven years old, making him a grade schooler. This was the key!

"I didn't know you wanted to be a teacher," Kio edged. Thank you, Kio. It's good to have wonderful friends!

"Regarding grade school educational practices," the sheet read.

What fortune to have majored in Japanese art! If I had tried to student teach Japanese language or math, or if the grade level of the class to which I was assigned had been different, then I would have had no chance of ever meeting Ritsuka. But in an art class, I would have the chance to meet all of the children in all the grades.

So what class was Ritsuka in? To ensure that I didn't make a bad impression on Ritsuka, on the off-chance that we might cross paths unexpectedly, I began to smile all over the place and interact with the children every single day. Before that, my smile hadn't gotten much use, so my facial muscles were awfully sore. But I endured because I felt such ascetic training was a prerequisite for meeting Ritsuka. *Oh, Ritsuka, I want to meet you soon.*

One day, as I cleaned up the art classroom, a blushing little girl came up to me and asked, "Are you in love with anyone, Mr. Agatsuma?" I answered her, beaming, because I was. Someone I loved very much!

It was one week later when I discovered that Ritsuka had transferred to another school.

END

ROSY DAYS (part 2)

by_Yutaka Kasami

In order to fulfill Seimei's final orders, his last will and testament, I decided to make contact with Ritsuka. To ensure that Ritsuka would not dislike me, or not be overly cautious of me, I planned to meet him in a natural manner and talk to him naturally. Gradually he would open up to me, and afterwards...

My Happy Life Plan (some would call it wicked) went to pieces when Ritsuka transferred to another school in the aftermath of Seimei's death. I spent a hellish two weeks at that school without Ritsuka.

What meaning did my time as a student teacher have? I probably looked like the world was ending, even as the clamor of school went on around me. Kio was happy to point out the damage done when I returned to the university from my student teacher duties looking like I was at death's door.

"What happened, Sou? You look awful! Tell me everything."

I figured that if I told him that Seimei was involved, Kio might get angry, so I left that part out and gave a simplified explanation.

"Huh...? You want to know how to get to know a child in a natural fashion?"

Kio dropped his head into his hands and gave me a look like I was the biggest pedophile on earth asking him how to score a Lolita of my own. "I guess the most natural relationship would be between a student and cram school teacher, or if you were a school teacher..." Apparently, Kio's imagination wasn't willing to fly very far from home base on this one. So I was back to where I started, where people my age had no point of contact with children. So how to meet Ritsuka?

"What about becoming the cool older guy in his neighborhood?" Kio joked. I got the sense he was speaking about something from his own childhood. The friendly, responsible big-brother type from the neighborhood... What a great idea!

I could start with "Good morning, hello, isn't it a nice day? Do you need any help with your homework?" That seemed normal enough. That seemed natural. I didn't grow up in an environment where I could get to know "people in the neighborhood," so if someone said it was normal, I'd believe them.

It felt like it could work. I was sure Ritsuka would open up to me! I really had to hand it to my best friend Kio!

As I immediately set out buying real estate magazines, Kio said, "Don't go stalking a grade schooler now, okay?"

In case Ritsuka were to ever come over, I rented a one-bedroom apartment (bedroom and living room), a bit larger than a small apartment, near the Aoyagi residence, in accordance with the information I received from Seimei. The rent was a bit high, but a smaller apartment would have been too cramped, only big enough for a bed and TV. Besides, if I were to welcome him to a room with only a bed, Ritsuka would put his guard up and probably never come back again.

Since I had few possessions, moving was easy. The hard part was living. You ask what was the hardest part? Throwing out the garbage every day! Some things were combustibles, other things were recyclables, and on and on. Everything I bought, I had to sort out in my mind how to properly dispose of.

"Mr. Agatsuma, these are non-combustibles." I gave a strained smile to the meddling housewife who liked to examine every piece of trash I put out.

"I'm sorry. I'll be more careful." I could not afford to let Soubi Agatsuma's reputation drop before even meeting Ritsuka. The effort was back in my smiles. This time I hoped to finally meet Ritsuka!

It was one week later when I discovered that Ritsuka had not only transferred to another school, but had moved away as well.

END

Whenever you run into a problem, solve it by saying "moving along."

loveless
FWAAAA
DU—H
RUSTL
IT'S GONE...

HOW COULD I HAVE LOST IT?
SHUF
SHUF
SHUF
IT MEANT A LOT TO ME!!
AND I JUST GOT IT TOO!!
SHUF
FW
IT'S GONE.
GONE.
GONE.
A
A
I CAN'T FIND IT ANY-WHERE !!
WHAT SHOULD I DO?!

HERE.
A PRESENT FOR YOU, RITSUKA.
I MADE IT. WILL IT GET IN THE WAY AS A CELL PHONE CHARM?
NO.
SO YOU'LL KEEP IT?
YEAH.
YAY! I MADE ONE FOR SOUBI TOO.
SOUBI DOESN'T NEED ONE.
Doesn't deserve it.
WHAT?
HEY, YUIKO...

WELL, IT'S JUST STUFF.
ACTUALLY ...
...I WISH I COULD GIVE YOU EVERY-THING, RITSUKA.
BUT...
...THIS IS ALL I HAVE TO GIVE.
HUH?
WHY DO YOU...
...GIVE ME THINGS?
AM I BEING ANNOYING ?!
EEK!
NO, NOT AT ALL.
IT'S NOT THAT AT ALL.
WOW...
THANKS.
It's hand-made ...!
I'LL TAKE GOOD CARE OF IT.

I CAN'T REMEMBER WHERE IT IS!!
AGH, I CAN'T BELIEVE MYSELF.
IT'S ONLY BEEN...
...ONE WEEK!
AND OF ALL THINGS, I STILL HAVE SOUBI'S.
GRP
AGH, I'M SO MAD!!
FIND IT. I HAVE TO FIND IT.
I HAVE TO FIND IT.
BUT WHERE DO I LOOK?!
I CAN'T EVER TELL YUIKO THAT I LOST IT.

MS. SHINO-NOME.
YOU DON'T EVEN HAVE AN UMBRELLA. YOU'LL CATCH COLD.
DID YOU LOSE SOME-THING?
SPSH
WHAT ARE YOU DOING?
URK!
RITSUKA!!
WHAT'S WRONG?
...
WHAT IS IT ?
I'LL HELP YOU FIND IT.
WAS IT SOME-THING VALU-ABLE?
LOOK AT YOU, YOU'RE ALL WET...
BECAUSE I WANT TO FIND IT...
MS. SHINO-NOME.
I'LL FIND IT BY MYSELF.
IT'S OKAY.
GUNG HO!
IS IT A KEY?
TO YOUR HOUSE? OR YOUR BICYCLE ?

IT'S REALLY ...
... REALLY ...
...IMPORTANT TO ME.
...BE BOUGHT WITH MONEY.
AND TO LOSE SOMETHING LIKE THAT...
...IS UNFOR-GIVABLE.
THE THINGS YUIKO GIVES ME...
...CAN NEVER...

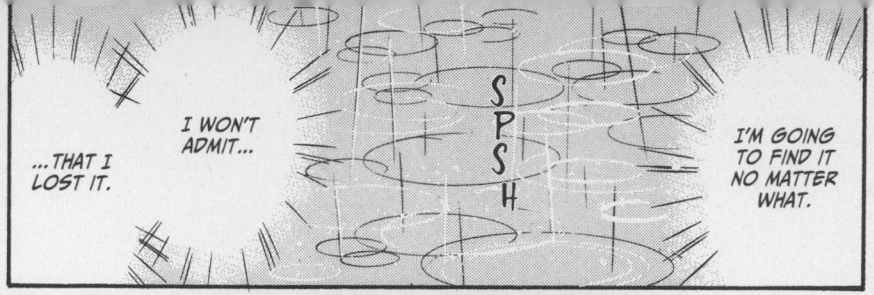
...THAT I LOST IT.
I WON'T ADMIT...
SPSH
I'M GOING TO FIND IT NO MATTER WHAT.

...I'LL JUST DIE!!!
SPLASH
IF I CAN'T FIND IT...

FWAA

HM?

AT LEAST I CAN LEND HIM A RAIN-COAT.
OH! I KNOW!

HE'S SO STUB-BORN.
OH...
OHH.
RIT-SUKA.
HE'S STILL SEARCH-ING. WHAT SHOULD I DO?
SPSH
SPSH
SPSH
HE'LL GET SICK.

AAAGH!!
PANIC!!
Y...
ZING
STOP IT, YOU'RE GONNA GET SICK.
ARE YOU LOOKING FOR YOUR CHARM?
RITSUKA?
WHAT ARE YOU DOING?
HERE.
IT'S OKAY... YOU DON'T HAVE TO.
AGHH
...!!
WHA...
AGHH
AGHH
CHK

AH...!!
THIS...
WHERE DID YOU FIND IT?!
YOU KNOW, I COULDN'T BELIEVE IT!
I FOUND IT ON THE BUS TODAY.
IT WAS STUCK IN THE BACK OF THE SEAT WHERE YOUR BUTT GOES.
THE BUS?!
THE SEAT AT THE VERY FRONT OF THE ROUND-TRIP BUS, WHERE YOU ALWAYS SIT, RITSUKA.
WHAT THE HECK?
I WAS SO SURPRISED.
SO...
I WAS THINKING THAT MAYBE YOU WERE LOOKING FOR IT.
YOU SHOULDN'T DO STUFF LIKE THIS. YOU'LL CATCH A COLD.

THANK GOD YOU FOUND IT!
BUT...
I'M SORRY.
...THAT I LOST IT.
IT DOESN'T CHANGE THE FACT...
HUH?
THAT'S OKAY. DON'T WORRY ABOUT IT.
...
EVERYTHING BREAKS OR GETS LOST SOMETIME.
YOU JUST HAVE TO TAKE CARE OF IT UNTIL THEN!

little loveless 2 / END

loveless....
I've been into this style lately!!
I have such a thing for
eye-patches and syringes,
even though I hate hospitals.
yun k 2002-2003

THANK YOU VERY MUCH!!!

I put everything I know to use in creating this mini fan comic.

My apologies to anyone who didn't like it.

Ahh, I just love manga so much. I love it! I love it to death!! There's much, much more, so if you like, please stay along for the ride.

Guest Yutaka Kagami!! Thank you very much for your short, short stories with clever punchlines. Soubi was such a dork that I burst out laughing.

Yun Kouga,
2002 winter
→2003

SEE YOU SOON!

Total sexual harassment!!

1♥2
END

YUN_KOUGA

began her career as a doujinshi author and debuted in 1986 with the original manga *Metal Heart*, serialized in *Comic VAL*. She is the creator of the popular series *Loveless* and *Earthian*, along with many manga and anime projects, including character design for *Gundam 00*. Her works *Crown of Love* and *Gestalt* are also published by VIZ.

Loveless

Volumes 1 + 2
VIZ Media Edition

Story and Art by YUN KOUGA

Translation // RAY YOSHIMOTO
English Adaptation // LILLIAN DIAZ-PRZYBYL
Touch-Up Art + Lettering // JAMES DASHIELL
Design // FAWN LAU
Editor // HOPE DONOVAN

Loveless © 2002-2003 by Yun Kouga
All rights reserved.
Original Japanese edition published by ICHIJINSHA, INC., Tokyo.
English translation rights arranged with ICHIJINSHA, INC.

The rights of the author(s) of the work(s) in this publication to be so identified have been asserted in accordance with the Copyright, Designs and Patents Act 1988. A CIP catalogue record for this book is available from the British Library.

The stories, characters and incidents mentioned in this publication are entirely fictional.

No portion of this book may be reproduced or transmitted in any form or by any means without written permission from the copyright holders.

Printed in the U.S.A.

Published by VIZ Media, LLC
P.O. Box 77010
San Francisco, CA 94107

10 9 8 7 6 5 4 3 2 1
First printing, October 2012

www.viz.com

IN THE NEXT VOLUME_3+4

Through a video game, Ritsuka tracks down the organization responsible for his brother's death, Septimal Moon. Meanwhile, Soubi fights against two separate units both calling themselves "Zero" and claiming to feel no pain.

D0666738

THIS IS THE END OF THE BOOK.

Loveless is printed from right to left in the original Japanese format in order to present Yun Kouga's art as it was meant to be seen.